THE COMING KINGDOM OF THE MESSIAH

A SOLUTION TO THE RIDDLE OF THE NEW TESTAMENT

Sir Anthony F. Buzzard, Bart., M.A. (Oxon.)

MINISTRY SCHOOL PUBLICATIONS
Wyoming, Michigan 49508

To my parents who taught me to ask questions; my wife, Barbara, and my daughters, Sarah and Claire, who share my excitement over the Messiah's Kingdom and allow me the luxury of thinking and writing; to hundreds of expert writers on theology whose competence in their specialized fields far exceeds mine; and to the Church of God (Abrahamic Faith) who have kept the light of truth burning for 160 years.

I am deeply indebted to members of the Southlawn Church of God (Abrahamic Faith) for their skill in preparing the manuscript for publication.

"This is in harmony with God's merciful purpose for the government of the world when the times are ripe for it—the purpose which He has cherished in His own mind of restoring the whole creation to find its one Head in Christ..." (Ephesians 1:9,10, Weymouth).

"...You were sacrificed, and with your blood you bought men for God of every race, language, people and nation, and made them a line of kings and priests, to serve our God and to rule the world" (Revelation 5:9,10, Jerusalem Bible).

Table of Contents

Foreword

Christians in New Testament times had a strong, clear hope for the future. They learned that hope when they accepted the Gospel—the Gospel of the Kingdom and the name of Jesus the Messiah (Luke 4:43, Acts 8:12, 28:23, 31, etc.).

A leading writer on the early church says that "without a coherent eschatology [an understanding of 'things to come' in the plan of God] it is not possible to do effective evangelism. The message of salvation must not only be related to the individual, the church and the Lord, but also to the whole purpose of God in His world" (Michael Green, *Evangelism in the Early Church*, p. 334).

The contemporary church does not have a coherent view of the future, and its message is correspondingly weakened. The problem lies simply in a loss of the New Testament Gospel of the Kingdom, a message which relates the believers to a definite goal, that of administering a New Order of society when Jesus returns. It is belief in Jesus as Messiah and in His messianic role as ruler of the world which animates the apostolic Christians; but the driving force of Messianism is absent from traditional theology and preaching. A revolution in thinking is needed for its recovery.

The message of the Kingdom has been generally dismissed as 'Jewish' or irrelevant in the scientific age. Ironically, though Jesus was a Jew, the theology of the church which has claimed His name has often demonstrated an anti-Semitic tendency. Hence the role of Jesus as the Messiah destined to rule in the future Kingdom has been obscured.

This book makes an appeal for a return to belief in the Gospel of the Kingdom and for a fresh reading of the New Testament which will allow its vibrant hope for the Messiah's Coming Kingdom to be rediscovered.

Introduction

Scholarship has reached an impasse in its attempt to understand the life and teaching of Jesus. Long established and deeply rooted patterns of thought prevent it from entering fully into the spirit of His mission. The difficulty lies quite simply in a lack of sympathy with the Messianic Kingdom which was the centre of all that Jesus taught.

The so-called problem of Jesus' messianic consciousness can be solved only when scholars abandon their prejudice against the Messianism which pervades the New Testament and indeed the entire Bible. The exposition of a religious document by those who do not share the beliefs set forth in the document presents enormous difficulties. Orthodox Christianity, both conservative and liberal, has very little time for things messianic, in the sense in which Jesus and His first century audience understood that term. Until expositors reorientate themselves to the Hebrew, messianic environment in which Jesus taught and react in sympathy with it, they will continue to obscure the one Jesus of history and faith, both the man and His message.

The process of reading the New Testament through the filter of church tradition has been going on for so long that nothing short of a theological revolution will bring it to an end. But there are hopeful signs. The late twentieth century has produced a mood likely to encourage the new look at the New Testament documents necessary for getting at the heart of them. A thirst for exploration is abroad among theologians and ordinary students of the Bible. There is evidence that the dogmas of post-biblical Christianity are beginning to relax their vice-like grip.

What needs to be undertaken urgently is a reading of the New Testament, and the whole Bible, allowing its unified message to speak to us. But we must be on guard against filtering out those elements of the message which we find distasteful or alien to our twentieth century ways of thinking. It has so often happened that scholars decide arbitrarily which elements of the New Testament they will accept as relevant to faith. If they do not care for apocalyptic, the Jesus they find in the records will not have said anything dramatic about the end of the age. If it is a liberal figure they are looking for, they will find him in Jesus. If a social reformer, they will discover him in the Christian documents.

It is widely recognized that this has been a weakness of the scholarly method in the past. Nevertheless, contemporary theologians continue to demonstrate their dislike of the Messianism of Jesus when they either ignore those of His sayings which prove Him to be in the best Old Testament and Jewish apocalyptic tradition, or blame all such "flights of fancy" on the New Testament church. Much ingenuity has been employed in an effort to excuse Jesus for those of His teachings which we find uncomfortable or unacceptable.

If, however, we read the New Testament in its Hebrew context, and allow ourselves to become involved in its message, we shall find that a Christianity emerges which is both coherent and practical, though different in some important respects from the faith which has gained acceptance as the religion of Jesus and the Apostles.

It is with the central theme of all Jesus' teachings that any investigation must begin. Fortunately scholarship is unanimous in its understanding of what that theme is. Even a cursory glance at the reports of Matthew, Mark and Luke reveal it to be unquestionably *the Kingdom of God*.

PART I

Jesus And The Messianic Future

1
The Heart of Christianity —
The Kingdom of God

Our Christian documents point to one undeniable fact: Jesus was concerned above all with the Kingdom of God. The Kingdom is the centre of His entire mission. It is His watchword and the nucleus of all His teaching. He announced that it was "at hand,"[1] demonstrated its power in His ministry, promised it as a reward to His disciples,[2] and urged them to pray for its coming.[3] He also assured His followers that they would one day occupy executive positions as ministers of state in the Kingdom:

> "You have stayed with me through all my trials; and just as my Father has given me the right to rule, so I will give you the same right. You will eat and drink at my table in my Kingdom, and you will sit on thrones to rule over the twelve tribes of Israel" (Luke 22:28-30, Good News Bible).

These momentous promises were to find fulfilment "in the New Age, when the Son of Man sits on His glorious throne" (Matt. 19:28). The promised New Age would arrive with the Second Coming.[4]

---

[1] Mark 1:14,15, "Jesus came into Galilee preaching the Gospel of God, and saying, 'the time is fulfilled, and the Kingdom of God is at hand; repent and believe in the Gospel.'"

[2] Luke 12:32, "Fear not little flock, for your Father has chosen gladly to give you the Kingdom."

[3] Matt. 6:10, "Thy Kingdom come, thy will be done on earth."

[4] Matt. 25:31, "When the Son of Man comes in His glory and all the angels with Him, then He will sit on His throne of glory."

Scholars are convinced that Jesus cannot be understood apart from the Kingdom of God. However, they are much less confident about their ability to offer a clear definition of the Kingdom. Theological writings often express uncertainty about whether we can ever recover the meaning which Jesus attached to the phrase "Kingdom of God":

"It is time someone called the bluff of those who think they know exactly what Jesus meant by the Kingdom of God" (Robert Morgan, in *Theology* , Nov., 1979 p. 458).

"Despite various attempts, it is not possible to define 'Kingdom of God' as it is used in the gospels or outside clearer than to say it stands for the sum total of blessing bestowed by God in Christ and consisting in the highest life in which we are yet truly at home" (*The New Century Bible*, Commentary on James, ed. E. M. Sidebottom, p. 41).

Other commentators sense that something is amiss when the phrase which Jesus used constantly is seldom, if ever, heard in Christian circles. Tom Sine points out that "the victory of the future of God was the central theme of the ministry of Jesus." Then he adds: "Michael Green asked during the Lausanne International Conference on World Evangelization in 1974, 'How much have you heard here about the Kingdom of God? Not much. *It is not our language.* But it was Jesus' prime concern'" (*The Mustard Seed Conspiracy*, pp. 102-3, emphasis added).

The frank admission of Peter Wagner is both disturbing as well as immensely instructive. In his book, *Church Growth and the Whole Gospel* (p. 2), he cites George Eldon Ladd as saying that "modern scholarship is quite unanimous in the opinion that the Kingdom of God was the central message of Jesus." Wagner then comments:

"If this is true, and I know of no reason to

dispute it, I cannot help wondering out loud why I haven't heard more about it in the thirty years I have been a Christian. I certainly have read about it enough in the Bible. Matthew mentions the Kingdom 52 times, Mark 19 times, Luke 44 times and John 4. But I honestly cannot remember any pastor whose ministry I have been under actually preaching a sermon on the Kingdom of God. As I rummage through my own sermon barrel, I now realize that I myself have never preached a sermon on it. Where has the Kingdom been?"[5]

Michael Green and Peter Wagner have put their fingers on a fundamental problem of Christianity as we know it. Contemporary evangelism and indeed preaching in general, though supposedly based on the Bible, do not sound like the teaching of Jesus. While they continue to use His name, they do not reflect His central theme—the Kingdom of God. This remarkable discrepancy was recognized also by the 19th century German theologian, Richard Rothe, who expressed his uneasiness about received methods of expounding the Bible:

"Our key does not open—the right key is lost and until we are put in possession of it again our exposition will never succeed. The system of biblical ideas *is not that of our schools* and so long as we attempt exegesis without it, the Bible will remain a half-closed book. We must enter upon it with other conceptions than those we have been accustomed to think the only possible ones" (Quoted by G. N. H. Peters, *The Theocratic Kingdom*, p. 21, emphasis added).

---

5   The centrality of the Kingdom of God in Jesus' teaching is emphasized in many contemporary sources, for example in *Christian Religious Education* by the Roman Catholic writer, Thomas Groome, pp. 35-55. In footnote 16 to chapter 5, he cites a number of leading contemporary scholars who agree that the Kingdom of God dominates everything that Jesus taught.

Our purpose is to show that the missing key which unlocks the message of Jesus, and indeed the whole Bible, is the Kingdom of God. The key, however, will be ineffective if it is bent out of shape. To make sense of what Jesus taught, we must understand the term "Kingdom of God" as He understood it. If we detach the Kingdom of God from its biblical context and attach to it a new meaning, we shall create a version of Christianity distorted at its very heart.

Without a grasp of the Kingdom, which is the axis around which all of Jesus' preaching and teaching revolves, we cannot hope to understand His message. The candid admissions of the scholars we have quoted suggest that Jesus' principal theme does not hold the central place in the teachings of the churches we call Christian. Indeed it is often omitted entirely! This can only mean that their systems of theology are in need of radical reformation.[6]

---

[6]   In an article entitled "Preaching the Kingdom of God," the British expositor, Dr. I. Howard Marshall of the University of Aberdeen, says: "During the past sixteen years I can recollect only two occasions on which I have heard sermons specifically devoted to the theme of the Kingdom of God.... I find this silence rather surprising because it is universaily agreed by New Testament scholars that the central theme of the teaching of Jesus was the Kingdom of God.... Clearly, then, one would expect the modern preacher who is trying to bring the message of Jesus to his congregation would have much to say about this subject. In fact my experience has been the opposite, and I have rarely heard about it" (*The Expository Times*, Oct. 1977, p. 13).

2
The Kingdom Expected by the Prophets

It must be significant that the Kingdom of God is the substance of the very first thing said about Jesus, even before His birth:

> *"The Lord God will give Him the throne of His father David and He will reign over the House of Jacob for ever; and His Kingdom will have no end" (Luke 1:32, 33).*

This announcement by the angel Gabriel came as no surprise as a description of the role of the Messiah. What the angel promised was exactly what the faithful were hoping for. If we ask what had prompted this hope, the answer is simply: the message of all the prophets. The recurrent theme of the Hebrew prophets is that the Kingdom of God will be established throughout the world with a rehabilitated Jerusalem as its capital and the Messiah as God's agent administering an ideal government. This promise of perfect government on earth receives the fullest treatment by the Hebrew prophets of the Old Testament. We may cite as typical of their vision of the future a selection from the numerous passages describing the reign of the promised descendant of David in a renewed earth. The expected world-empire would be God's Kingdom administered for Him by His unique representative and vice-regent, the Messiah.[7]

---

[7] The fact of the future Kingdom promised by the prophets is well known to standard authorities on biblical theology: "A constant feature in the eschatological picture of the Old Testament is Israel's restoration to its own land.... The question

> *"A throne will even be established in lovingkindness and a judge [an administrator] will sit on it in faithfulness in the tent of David; moreover he will seek justice and be prompt in righteousness"* (Isaiah 16:5).

The simplicity of the concept is well captured by the same verse as translated by the Good News Bible:

> *"Then one of David's descendants will be King and he will rule the people with faithfulness and love. He will be quick to do what is right, and he will see that justice is done."*

What the prophets saw was a vision of utopian conditions on earth, following the conquest of the world by Yahweh (the Lord God) acting through His chosen agent, the promised King:

> *"The Lord of Hosts will reign on Mount Zion and in Jerusalem"* (Isaiah 24:23).

> *"He [the Messiah] will speak peace to the nations and His dominion will be from sea to sea, and from the River [Euphrates] to the end of the earth"* (Zechariah 9:10).

Obadiah describes the supremacy of Israel in the coming messianic rule:

---

how in our day we are to interpret such prophecies is a double one. It is a question, first, of what the prophets meant. And to this question there can be but one answer—*their meaning is the literal sense of their words.* They spoke of the people of Israel and of the land of Canaan and predicted the restoration of the people to their land.... There is no question as to the meaning of the Old Testament prophecies; the question is how far this meaning is now valid." (*Hastings Dictionary of the Bible,* art. Eschatology, Vol. 1, p. 737, emphasis added). The real question, however, is whether we are prepared to believe the prophets. What the prophets predicted is clear. The problem is that the churches do not believe what they wrote! (Cp. Acts 26:27, where Paul challenged Agrippa with the question: "Do you believe the prophets?")

"The community of Jacob will regain territory from those who took it from them. They will recover the Negev from Mount Esau and the Shephelah from the Philistines. They will regain the region of Ephraim and Gilead. The exiles of the people of Israel will annex Canaanite territory as far as Zaraphath. The exiles who were in Sepharad will reclaim the Negev towns. Then governors will go up to Mount Zion to govern Mount Esau, and the Kingdom will be the Lord's" (Obadiah 17, 19, 20, translation based on the version in the *New International Commentary on the Old Testament*, by J. C. Allen).

Evidently the Kingdom of God is to be a new political and territorial order with its headquarters in the promised land of Israel. This is the unanimous view of all the prophets. Jeremiah, too, had recorded the words of the Lord promising national restoration for Israel under the Messiah:

"Behold the days are coming, declares the Lord, when I shall raise up for David a righteous branch and he will reign as king and act wisely and do justice and righteousness in the land. In his days Judah will be saved and Israel shall dwell securely" (Jer. 23:5-6).

Isaiah's and Micah's vision is no less clearly defined, with the additional guarantee of multilateral disarmament under the government of the Messiah:

"A child will be born to us, a son will be given to us; and the government will rest on His [the promised deliverer, the Messiah's] shoulders.... There will be no end to the increase of His government or peace, on the throne of David and over his kingdom, to establish it and uphold it with righteousness from then on forevermore.... The law will go forth from Zion and the word of the Lord from

Jerusalem and He will judge between the nations and will render decisions for many peoples. And they will hammer their swords into ploughshares and their spears into pruning hooks. Nation will not lift up sword against nation. And never again will they train for war" (Isaiah 9:6,7; 2:3,4; Micah 4:2,3).

One of the clearest descriptions of the Kingdom of God appears in Daniel 2:44. Following the destruction of hostile world powers, "the God of Heaven will set up a Kingdom [clearly here a world empire] which will never be destroyed, and that Kingdom will not be left for another people; it will crush and put to an end all these kingdoms, but it will itself endure for ever." In Daniel 7 the same promised Kingdom is to be administered by the Son of Man (Jesus' favourite self-designation) and His followers, God's chosen people:

"And to him [the Son of man] was given a dominion, glory and a Kingdom, that all the peoples, nations and men of every language might serve Him. His dominion is an everlasting dominion, which will not pass away; and his Kingdom is one which will not be destroyed.... Then the power and greatness of all the kingdoms under the whole heaven will be given to the people of the supreme God. Their royal power will never end and all rulers on earth will serve and obey them" (Dan. 7:14,27, Good News Bible).

The revolution associated with the Messiah's instalment in His Kingdom is described by Zechariah:

"The Lord will go forth and fight against those nations...and in that day the Lord will be king over all the earth.... Then it will come about that any who are left of all the nations that went against Jerusalem will go up

from year to year to worship the King, the
Lord of Hosts" (Zechariah 14:3,9,16).

These and many other passages in the prophets
demonstrate beyond dispute that the Kingdom of God
was to be a new world government on earth, administered by the Messiah, God's chosen King, assisted by a
group of associates called in Daniel "the Saints of the
Most High" (7:27). The picture of a restored earth is
common to all the prophets. It is the basis of the
messianic hope summed up by the term "Kingdom of
God."

3
Traditional Jewish and Christian Explanations

Taking their cue from this unified expectation of the prophets, the Jewish rabbis gathered from their scriptures the following information about the Messiah and His future Kingdom:

1. The Messiah is to be a descendant of the house of David and his purpose is to restore the Kingdom to Israel and extend it over the world.
2. In a last terrible battle for world domination the enemies of God, concentrated in a single Antichrist, will be defeated and destroyed.
3. The establishment of Messiah's Kingdom, following the defeat of Antichrist, will result in the spiritual and political hegemony of Israel, when all the nations will be taught to accept the unity of God, acknowledge the rule of His representative, the Messiah, and seek instruction from the law.

It is beyond question that the source of this information is the Hebrew Old Testament scriptures. It is no less clear that the hope kindled by the prophets was fully confirmed by Gabriel when he designated Jesus as the promised ruler in whom the long-expected worldwide government would be realized:

> "The Lord God will give him the throne of his father David and he will reign over the house of Jacob for ever" (Luke 1:32,33).

Luke has given us in these verses a definitive Christian statement, on the highest authority, about the destiny of Jesus. He is to restore the fortunes of His people and rule the world from Jerusalem as the divinely appointed king. The hope was social, spiritual and political - and related *to the earth!* Belief in the coming Kingdom was the heart of New Testament Christianity as Luke, the traveling companion of Paul, taught it to Theophilus (Luke 1:1-4).

In the light of the unanimous message of the Hebrew prophets, the Jewish people have generally concluded that Jesus' claim to Messiahship should be rejected. They argue as follows:

> Since the claim to be Messiah implies that one will overthrow the world powers, and since Jesus did not overturn the Roman power in Palestine or establish the Kingdom of God, Jesus and His disciples were wrong in believing that He was the promised Messiah. The New Testament documents therefore present a false claim.

Faced with the same data, traditional Christianity has reasoned like this:

> Since Jesus claimed to be and was indeed the Messiah, and since the Roman rule in Palestine was not overturned and the Messianic Kingdom was not established on the earth, Jesus cannot have intended to carry out the messianic programme as the Jews expected. He must therefore have so reinterpreted the messianic hope of the prophets as to exclude any idea of *political* revolution and the establishment of messianic government on earth.

To support this line of reasoning, theologians have expended a great deal of scholarly energy in an effort to convince us that the Jewish understanding of the Kingdom and Jesus' conception of it were irreconcilably opposed. Above all we are not to think that Jesus had any political ambition. His objectives, so it has long been maintained, were entirely 'spiritual.'

The gist of this longstanding and deeply entrenched conviction can be summarized as follows:

> Many in Israel were expecting salvation through a Messiah, an anointed one, whom God would send to rule an earthly kingdom. This Messiah would bring glory to Israel, destroying evil and establishing righteousness with irresistible power. What Jesus did was quite different. He established the Kingdom in the hearts of His followers.

Standard works constantly reflect the same view of Jesus and the Kingdom. Common to all of them, at least, is the recognition that the Kingdom of God was the basis of all that Jesus taught. But the Kingdom, far from being a world government, is reduced to an ethical rule of God in the hearts of men:

> "The burden of Jesus' message was: the Kingdom of God is the will of the heavenly Father enthroned in the hearts of men. He taught that faith in God would bring in a new order of things in which the cares and fears of life would be abandoned.... By prayer from hearts which have been purified through repentance and sincere desire of a better life, the presence of God will be gained, His Kingdom will come and the reward of men will be fellowship with God" (*New Age Encyclopedia*, Vol. 6, pp. 176, 177).

Astonishingly, this sort of description of the Kingdom of God has been accepted by the church-going public as a satisfactory reflection of the Kingdom which appears in the Christian documents. Yet the popular view omits any reference to the *second* coming of Jesus and the subsequent Messianic Kingdom on earth. Moreover, the standard definition of the Kingdom is open to a major objection: it is utterly self-contradictory to claim to be the Messiah and at the same time to reject altogether the *political* role which the Hebrew scriptures designate for the Messiah and which is the main point of Messiahship! It makes no sense at all that Jesus could speak of the Kingdom of God (and of Himself as Messiah) while denying the meaning of that phrase as the restoration of a world-wide theocratic government on earth, with Jerusalem as the metropolis of a new society, as all the Hebrew prophets had envisaged it. The rejection of the external, political Kingdom is all the more impossible when one constantly affirms, as Jesus did, that the Hebrew scriptures are the inspired and authoritative source of all religious truth.   Since no new political order on earth appeared as a result of Jesus' ministry, commentators have chosen between two alternatives: either Jesus did not in fact ever claim to be the Messiah, in which case His disciples must have mistakenly attributed that title to Him; or He did indeed claim to be the Messiah, but used the title and the phrase "Kingdom of God" in a radically new way which divorced it for ever from its Old Testament roots, above all divesting it of any political significance.

4
A Third Solution

Neither of these solutions does justice to the evidence of the biblical documents. In both cases large sections of the available data are simply not being taken into account. The suggestion that Jesus did not in fact claim to be the Messiah would render the whole New Testament fraudulent. But it is no less problematic to argue that Jesus abandoned the Jewish, Old Testament national hope for a worldwide messianic government, foreseen by all the prophets. Ample evidence exists in the New Testament to show that He did no such thing. There remains, therefore, a third option. With His contemporaries, Jesus normally used the phrase "Kingdom of God" to describe the new political order on earth promised by sacred scripture, but He and His Apostles sometimes extended the term to include a preliminary stage in the activity of the Kingdom:

1. His announcement of the Messianic Kingdom of God in advance of its establishment worldwide at Jesus' return to the earth in power and glory.
2. A demonstration of the Kingdom's power invested in Jesus, and His chosen followers, manifested in their healing and exorcism.
3. The recruiting of disciples through Jesus' ministry and their training for leadership in the coming Messianic Kingdom, as well as participation in the announcement of the Kingdom prior to its coming.
4. The death of the Messiah for the sins of the world.

5. His ascension and session at the right hand
   of the Father (as predicted by the all-
   important Psalm 110:1)[8] pending His return
   to inaugurate the Kingdom as the renewed
   social and political order on earth.

It is important to note that these preliminary de-
velopments in the progress of the Kingdom were not
clearly distinguished by the Old Testament prophets
from the full establishment of the Kingdom worldwide,
though in retrospect we can see plain indications of
the two phases of the divine programme scattered
throughout Old Testament scripture. In traditional
Christianity, talk of the Kingdom of God as in some
sense a description of the Christian life *now* has overshadowed, to the point of obscuring and even eliminat-
ing, the Kingdom as the establishment of the divine
rule worldwide, which for Jesus and the whole New
Testament, as well as for the prophets, *is to be the
great event precipitated by His Second Coming.*[9]

The Kingdom taught by Jesus is first and foremost the new order on earth associated with a great
future crisis in history, to be marked by His return in
power. For Jesus the Kingdom had not yet come. Its
coming is to be prayed for![10] Certainly the power of

---

[8] This verse is cited or alluded to in the New Testament more
than any other Old Testament passage. It is obviously of the
greatest importance for our understanding of apostolic Christianity.

[9] Cp. *The Century Bible,* Introduction to Thessalonians, p. 29:
"It has been recently argued that the Kingdom of God was the
principal topic in the teaching of Jesus, who whenever He spoke
of the Kingdom of God meant that triumphant new order of the
future which would be set up on His return to this world in
glory with the angels." The reference is to Johannes Weiss's
*Predigt Jesu vom Reiche Gottes (Jesus' preaching about the
Kingdom of God),* 1892. Weiss rightly saw that Jesus spoke
always of a real kingdom of the future. He then proceeded to
tell us that such teaching was irrelevant for us now!

[10] Matt. 6:10, "Thy Kingdom come."

the Kingdom had been displayed in His ministry, but this was only a foretaste of the coming of the Kingdom, which still lay in the future, and depended entirely on the return of Jesus, as King, to set it up.

If the New Testament is read from a perspective which allows for *both* a present preliminary manifestation of the Kingdom as well as its future worldwide establishment at the Second Coming, it becomes clear that Jesus never for one moment deprived the Kingdom of God of the political and territorial significance given to it by the prophets and incorporated into Jewish religion as the nation's great hope. Jesus did not, however, *at his first coming* expect to introduce the Messianic Kingdom politically. Nevertheless, all His teaching was directed towards preparing His followers for the future arrival of the Messianic Kingdom. At the end of His ministry He submitted Himself to crucifixion at the hands of the Roman and Jewish authorities, promising that He would return after resurrection and an interval unspecified, to inaugurate the Kingdom politically and universally, thus fulfilling in every detail the predictions of all Old Testament prophecy, as well as vindicating His claim to Messiahship. "

---

[11] Cp. *The Century Bible Commentary*, Introduction to Thessalonians, p. 30: "What the Jews looked for at the first coming of Christ, the Christians were inclined to look for at the Second Coming."

5
The Non-Political Messiah of Traditional Christianity

Traditional versions of Christianity have been curiously reluctant to acknowledge the political dimension of Jesus' teaching. Commentators have laboured to exclude it, employing a battery of different devices to explain it away. This process has involved nothing less than a tour de force by which the plainest biblical statements have been emptied of their obvious meaning.

These techniques have not escaped criticism from those expositors who realized that violence was being done to the sacred text. The remark of Albert Schweitzer deserves to be quoted in this context:

"Many of the greatest sayings [of Jesus] are found lying in a corner like explosive shells, from which the charges have been removed....We have made Jesus hold another language with our time from that which he really held" (*Quest of the Historical Jesus*, p. 400).

Schweitzer was persuaded that Jesus' sense of crisis and the end of the world represented the very heart of His mind and message and that our records do not make any sense unless they are seen in this light.

Another commentator, David Baron, complained that the words of the prophets had been mishandled by expositors in a way which eliminated the reality of the future Kingdom of God. What Baron says of the commentaries on the prophet Zechariah applies equally well to much traditional treatment of the Kingdom of God in the teaching of Jesus:

"Almost all the existing works on this prophetic book are in one way or another defective,
and some of them are even misleading. The
older commentaries, though commendable for
their reverent spiritual tone and practical teaching, and some of them containing a good deal of
sound philological and historical material, are
more or less vitiated by the allegorizing
principle of interpretation by means of which
*all reference to a concrete Kingdom of God on
earth, a literal restoration of Israel and
the visible appearing and reign of Messiah are
explained away*" (*The Prophecies of Zechariah,*
pp. viii, ix, emphasis added).

Since the Kingdom of God was the heart of all
that Jesus taught, and since He fully endorsed the
hopes of the prophets, [12] the removal of the Messianic
Kingdom will threaten the substance of the Christian
message. The untold damage done by the "allegorizing
principle of interpretation" (a sophisticated phrase for
"explaining away") has not been limited to the book of
Zechariah. Almost all standard commentaries on the
New Testament are defective for the reason stated by
David Baron. The teaching of Jesus suffered a devastating blow when expositors no longer acknowledged
that the Kingdom of God means primarily and domi-
nantly what it had always meant to the prophets: "a
concrete Kingdom of God on the earth" to be initiated
by the event known in the Old Testament as the Day
of the Lord and in the New as the Second Coming of
Jesus. [13] The usual meaning of the term "Kingdom of
God" on Jesus' lips is the new order to be inaugurated
by His return. This corresponds exactly with the Old

---

[12]   Matt. 5:17, "Think not that I have come to destroy the law
or the prophets." Rom. 15:8, "Jesus Christ was a minister to
the circumcision to confirm the promises made to the Fathers."

[13]   See for example I Thess. 5:2, II Thess. 2:2, I Cor. 1:8, II
Cor. 1:14. The day of the Lord is the same as the Day of
Christ's future coming.

Testament's descriptions of God reigning (i.e., in the person of His chosen King, the Messiah).[14] Traditional theology seems to have forgotten that Jesus came to "confirm the promises made to the Fathers" (Rom. 15:8), and the Fathers, beginning with Abraham, were expecting to "inherit the world" (Rom. 4:13). The promises made to Abraham, which the New Testament endorses, were based on the hope of taking charge of the earth (cp. Jesus' reward to His disciples: "Be thou in authority over ten cities" - Luke 19:17). The hope kindled by Jesus is no different. He promised the meek that they would one day "inherit the earth" (Matthew 5:5), and that God would then "give them the Kingdom" (Luke 12:32). *New Testament Christianity promises its adherents administrative positions in a new government destined to appear on earth when Jesus returns.*

A Messiah who fails to take up his office as ruler of a universal empire centred in Jerusalem is not the Messiah expected by the prophets and promised by Gabriel to Mary (Luke 1:32-35). It is fair to ask, therefore, whether the Jesus of traditional theology, of whom little or nothing is ever said in regard to a world empire on earth inaugurated by a future crisis, can be the Jesus Messiah of the Bible.

---

14   See, in addition to many other passages, Isa. 52:7-10, 32:1, Ps. 2, Zech. 14:9ff.

6
The Future Political Kingdom in the Teaching of Jesus

A number of critically important sayings of Jesus have not received the attention they deserve. These are verses which demonstrate that Jesus was very much conscious of the political nature of the Kingdom which as Messiah he was destined to administer upon His return at the end of the age.

Anyone claiming to be the promised Son of David could not have failed to be impressed by the fundamental importance of the covenant made with David, described in II Samuel 7 (parallel to I Chron. 17). [15] As is well known, this formed the basis of God's promise to bring about peace on earth through His chosen King. [16] It was widely recognized from a reading of the Hebrew scriptures that the glory of David's kingdom would eventually be restored to Israel, with benefits for the whole world, when the Messiah entered upon His reign. Thus it was that prominent disciples of Jesus were eagerly awaiting the "consolation of Israel" not only before Jesus' birth, but after He had completed His brief ministry in Palestine. The national expectation of the messianic reign remains central to the Christian records: the righteous and devout Simeon was "looking for the consolation of Israel and the holy spirit was upon him" (Luke 2:26). Anna the prophetess, commended by Luke for her

---

[15]   The importance of this covenant is seen in the references to it in Pss. 72, 89, and Luke 1:32-35.

[16]   This divine intervention is vividly described in the Psalms, especially Pss. 2 and 110. Both the Qumran community and the Christians saw the application of II Sam. 7:14 to the promised deliverer (Heb. 1:5, Luke 1:35).

exceptional devotion to God, was "looking for the redemption of Jerusalem" (Luke 2:38). Joseph of Arima-
thea, whom Matthew describes as a disciple of Jesus
(Matt. 27:57), was "a good and honourable man who
was waiting for the Kingdom of God" (Luke 23:51).
This was after Jesus' death. He evidently did not
believe the Kingdom had come with the ministry of
Jesus even though, certainly, the records describe His
ministry as an anticipation of the Kingdom (Matt. 11:5).

Likewise, the thief on the cross recognized the
certainty of the future coming of the Kingdom when
he pleaded with Jesus for a part in it:

> "Lord, remember me when you come into
> [i.e., to inaugurate] your Kingdom" (Luke
> 23:42).

Precisely the same enthusiasm for the Kingdom
had prompted the request by the mother of James and
John on behalf of her children. Her petition reveals
the biblical Christian idea of the Messianic Kingdom,
and Jesus did nothing at all to disturb her understanding of the kind of kingdom this would be:

> "Command that in your kingdom these two
> sons of mine may sit, one on your right hand
> and one on your left" (Matt. 20:21).

The kingdom she had in mind was certainly not
limited to a kingdom in the heart. Jesus' reply confirmed that the honour of sitting in a principal place
in the Kingdom was reserved "for those for whom it
has been prepared" (Mark 10:40). Moreover, He added
that greatness in the coming Kingdom of God is for
those who first accept the role of a servant, as He
Himself had done (Mark 10:42-45, cp. Phil. 2:6-8). But
there is no question in Jesus' mind about the nature
of the future Kingdom, nor about status in it. The
disciples were not rebuked for any misunderstanding
about the fact of a future Kingdom in which positions
could be held. They needed only to learn that the
path to greatness lay through humility and servanthood.

The question of the Christian goal is immensely important in the records of Jesus' teaching. The Apostles were instructed by Jesus to recognize the promised Messianic Kingdom as the heart of the New Covenant. For them the supreme objective of the Christian life was to assist the Messiah in the administration of His Kingdom. At the last supper, He said to them:

> *"I covenant with you, just as my Father has covenanted with me, to grant you a kingdom that you may eat and drink at my table in my kingdom, and you will sit on thrones administering the twelve tribes of Israel" (Luke 22:28-30).*

Only a few moments earlier Jesus had said that He would not drink the wine of the Passover with them again until the Passover would be "fulfilled in the Kingdom of God," that is "until the Kingdom of God *comes*" (Luke 22:16,18). Then they would eat and drink in His presence, reunited with Him, as executives of the Kingdom. This glorious occasion was to be "in the New Age [literally, "when the world is reborn"] when the Son of Man sits on His throne of glory" (Matt. 19:28).

The Apostles were in no doubt about when this would be, for Jesus also said:

> *"When the Son of Man comes,* **then** *He will sit on His throne of glory" (Matt. 25:31).*

The implications of all this are clear for all to read. There will be a Kingdom inaugurated by the return of Christ at the beginning of the New Age. There will be thrones and government over the twelve tribes regathered in the land. And there will be fellowship with Jesus in that New Age, a fellowship not to be renewed "until the Kingdom comes" (Luke 22:18).

While this information about the Kingdom of God forms the framework of all that Jesus taught, how far does it play any part at all in what we have come to call Christianity?

7
The Departing and Returning Nobleman

On another occasion Jesus had thrown further light on the Kingdom of God by comparing Himself to a nobleman who was destined to depart and later return to take charge of His Father's Kingdom. Jesus told this parable in order to clarify, in the simplest terms, the stages of the divine plan in history. Since He and His disciples were in the vicinity of Jerusalem, approaching the city which everyone recognized would be the capital of the Kingdom, His audience—many of whom had accepted His claim to Messiahship—very reasonably expected "that the Kingdom of God was going to appear immediately" (Luke 19:11).

Luke's account leaves us in no doubt that the Kingdom of God under discussion was a kingdom based in Jerusalem, and the geographical proximity of the king to the capital prompted the excitement that the hopes of the prophets and the nation were now finally to be realized. The parable which followed was to teach the lesson that the Kingdom was not to appear *immediately*. That it would appear eventually was not in question. Moreover its appearance would mean the destruction of Jesus' enemies:

> *"These enemies of mine, who did not want me to reign over them, bring them here and slay them in my presence" (Luke 19:27).*

Not for one moment did Jesus suggest that the people had misunderstood the nature of the Kingdom, or that they should look only for a kingdom "in the heart." By means of a simple story about the nobleman, He made it clear that the Kingdom of God would not be

publicly inaugurated until He returned from heaven after having received from the Father His royal authority. At His return He would exercise His royal power
by executing His enemies for refusal to submit to His
sovereignty (Luke 19:27). At the same time His faithful followers were to be rewarded for their productive
service while the master had been absent, by being
put in charge of urban populations in the Kingdom
(Luke 19:17).

The parable made perfect sense as a confirmation
of what the celebrated Psalm 2 had predicted of the
Messiah, the Lord's anointed. According to this
Psalm, God has promised to give His Messiah "the
nations as His inheritance and the very ends of the
earth as His possession" (v. 8). The king was to
"break them with an iron rod and shatter them like
earthenware" (v. 9). In the same Psalm the world
rulers whom the Messiah confronted at His return
were urged to "do homage to the Son, lest He become
angry and destroy you" (v. 12). Both the Jews and
Jesus recognized in Psalm 2 a forecast of the Messiah's
conquest of the world at His arrival in power. In
Jesus, the Christian community saw "a male child who
is to rule the nations with a rod of iron" (Rev. 12:5).
Indeed the challenge to a position of "authority over
the nations" was designed by the risen Jesus to spur
the faithful on to the end (Rev. 2:26). [17]

---

[17] See Rev. 11:15, 12:5, 12:10, 19:15 for the application of
Psalm 2 to Jesus; also Acts 4:25, 13:33, the latter reference
being to the conception of Jesus. Acts 13:34 speaks of His
resurrection.

8
Jesus,
the Jewish-Christian Messiah

The data we have examined reveals a Jesus who is a thoroughly political figure, though he wielded none of his political authority *at His first coming,* and kept Himself and His followers strictly apart from the politics of the day. [18]   He demonstrated in His ministry the qualities of tenderness and compassion which justify his claim to reflect the character of His Father.   The contrast between the suffering servant who later becomes the conquering king shows the extraordinary range of the personality of Jesus.   In the first century He did not "quarrel nor cry out...a battered reed He will not break off and a smouldering wick He will not put out" (Matt. 19,20).   Nor did He then make judgments on secular matters; but at His return in glory He is destined to judge the nations and rule them with a rod of iron (Rev. 19:15).   Any portrait which does not allow the colours of both aspects of the Messiah's activity is hopelessly distorted.   Belief in the Jesus of history, who is of necessity also the Jesus of faith, must be based on the full range of revealed truth about Him.

Traditional Christian teaching has almost entirely discarded the political element in the teaching of Jesus, either by neglecting the sayings about rulership

---

[18]   There is a sense in which Jesus' mission was thoroughly political from the start.   The New Testament describes Him as battling with the supernatural forces of Satan.   It would be proper to call this involvement in "cosmic politics."   For biblical Christianity the battle between Jesus and Satan is the real issue.   And it is a struggle for world domination yet to be resolved, though the promise of Jesus' ultimate triumph is assured.

which He expected for Himself and His disciples, or
by claiming, against the plainest evidence of the New
Testament, that the executive positions promised to
His disciples were to be assumed *now*, before the Second Coming. The theory that the Apostles were of-
fered kingship over the *Church* is in collision with the
clear teaching of the New Testament that it is "in the
New Age when Jesus comes in His glory" (Matt. 19:28,
25:31), and not before, that the Messiah's followers
are to share rulership with Him. The nobleman in the
parable had to return from heaven before he was
authorised to deal with His enemies and rule with the
faithful in His Kingdom. Until Jesus comes back the
disciples are to persist in praying "Thy Kingdom
come," and it is not until "the Kingdom comes" (Luke
22:18) that Jesus sits down with His disciples in the
Kingdom in which He promises them a share.

The widely held view that the promise of rulership applies to the period *prior to* the Second Coming
represents a fatal dislocation of the biblical scheme,
and has had the tragic effect of promoting an entirely
unbiblical view of the future and drawing a veil
over the reality of the Kingdom of God to be put
into office when Jesus returns. The mind of Jesus is
fully revealed in the Revelation which He communi-
cated through the beloved disciple John. We find Him
corroborating His exhortation to persist until the Great
Day:

> *"Hold fast until I come. To those who*
> *win the victory, who continue to the end to*
> *do what I want, I will give the same author-*
> *ity that I received from my Father: I will*
> *give them authority over the nations, to rule*
> *them with an iron rod, and to break them in*
> *pieces like clay pots....To those who win the*
> *victory I will give the right to sit beside*
> *me on my throne, just as I have been victor-*
> *ious and sit by my Father on His throne"*
> *(Rev. 2:26, 3:21).*

These are the words of the Saviour Himself (Rev. 2:18—"The Son of God...says this"), and the churches are exhorted to "hear what the Spirit says to them." It is hard to see how the average church-goer possesses anything like the outlook on the future inculcated by Jesus in these verses. Traditional Christianity appears to have made nothing of these central Christian teachings. The words we have cited in Revelation are, after all, only a confirmation of what Jesus had already laid before the Apostles as the goal of their discipleship—to join Him in administering a renewed Israel and the world (Matt. 19:28, Luke 22:28-30, Rev. 2:26, 3:21).

Despite the fact that this full-blooded messianic hope was instilled by Jesus, commentators have expressed their antipathy to His Messianism by labeling the activity of the Messiah described in Psalm 2 and echoed in Jesus' words in Revelation as "unchristian." They do not see how the activity of the king described in Psalm 2 can have any relevance to Jesus. Despite His own quotation of Psalm 2 with reference to Himself and His church, the following comment is not untypical:

> "Psalm 2 cannot be strictly regarded as referring to Jesus, partly because the establishment of the King upon the holy hill of Zion would have no relevance in His case; partly because the conception of His function as dashing His enemies in pieces is unchristian" [19] (*Dictionary of Christ and the Gospels*, Vol. II, p. 452).

Theologians who canvass this point of view are caught in a tragic contradiction. While they say that they accept Jesus as the Christ, they attempt to circumscribe His activities in a way which would exclude

---

[19]   At the Second Coming Jesus will act as the agent of God's wrath against a hostile world. Meanwhile Christians are required to deal non-violently with their enemies (Matt. 5:39, 44).

a major part of biblical messiahship. Jesus does not share the qualms of the theologians about the second Psalm, for in the Revelation which He granted to John, and through him to the church, He actually urges the faithful to press on to the goal which is to share messianic "authority over the nations." The promises of royal privilege are clear beyond any dispute in Revelation 2:26 and 3:21, as they are in Matt. 19:28 and Luke 22:28-30 (quoted earlier). In Rev. 3:21 Jesus carefully distinguishes between His present coordination with the Father on the Father's throne and His future reign on His own throne in the Messianic Kingdom: "I will give them the right to sit beside me on my throne, just as I have been victorious and sit by my Father on His throne." All this is precisely what we anticipate from Jesus' teaching in the Gospels and from the Old Testament which Jesus accepted as the authoritative word of God.

The recognition and acceptance of the messianic tone of Jesus' preaching of the Kingdom will throw an entirely new light on His person and ministry. It is widely recognized that our understanding of "last things" (eschatology) has somehow fallen into a state of confusion, with the most brilliant of commentators apparently doing their best to be rid of the whole problem of the future. It is important to realize that confusion over the future means confusion over the Gospel of Jesus which is inextricably bound up with an apocalyptic view of history, a view which sees the whole challenge of human existence in a striving towards participation in the Kingdom of God to be manifested in the New Age inaugurated by the Second Coming. Once it is seen that the Old Testament apocalyptic hope for a final divine intervention in the affairs of our world remains undiminished in the New Testament, theology will return to proclaiming the message of Jesus about the Kingdom of God rather than using an extraordinary armoury of critical devices designed apparently to dismiss from the teaching of Jesus anything that cannot be harmonized with "our modern scientific view."

9
The Undefined Future Kingdom of Traditional Christianity

In the teaching of Jesus the future is always prominent and the present is meaningful as a preparation for the end of the age when Jesus returns. Any theology which does not operate within this framework has lost its foundation in the Bible.

Scholarship recognizes that Jesus spoke of the Kingdom of God as future and yet as in some sense present. Beyond this it seems reluctant to go. It has not defined what is meant by the *future* Kingdom. This vagueness about the Kingdom leads automatically to a vagueness about the Gospel—which is the Gospel of the Kingdom—and threatens to obscure the whole Christian message.

The New Testament is not silent, as we have seen, about the future Kingdom. If it only occasionally spells out the details of the future theocracy of the Messiah in which the Church is to take part as executives with Christ, this is because it assumes that the doctrine of the Kingdom will be understood from the Old Testament. It never hints that the much greater detail provided by the prophets has been superseded. All that the prophets had revealed about the future Kingdom and the reign of the Messiah awaits fulfilment at the coming of Jesus in glory. The hope for the restoration of Israel is everywhere implied as part of the Christian heritage which Jesus never questioned. This was particularly clear from Jesus' promise to the Apostles that they will preside over the twelve tribes in the New Age (Matt. 19:28). The idea does not originate in the New Testament. The Psalmist had foreseen a time when regathered

Israel would live in peace under the administration of
the "thrones of the House of David" (Psalm 122:5).
Isaiah had spoken of Jerusalem restored to perfection,
her administrators purified "as at the first" (Isa. 1:26),
and of an ideal King ruling with his princes (Isa. 32:1).
In the New Testament the Book of Revelation quite
deliberately and specifically gathers together the
strands of messianic prophecy and relates them to the
Second Coming. It is the Christian Apocalypse. How
can it be anything else since its author is Jesus
Christ? (Rev. 1:1) To speak of the Apocalypse as
"Jewish," as if this means it is not therefore Christian,
is fundamentally confusing. Christianity is itself
thoroughly Jewish. Jesus is a Jew whose teaching is
rooted in the heritage of Israel. In the Book of
Revelation He confirms much of what had been
already recorded in the Gospels. Jesus' exhortations
to the churches in Revelation 2 and 3 show that He
subscribed wholeheartedly to the traditional Messianism
of the Old Testament. This fact cannot be avoided
except by the drastic expedient of denying the author-
ship of the Revelation to the risen Christ and excising
a mass of apocalyptic sayings from the gospels.

It is the tragedy of critical scholarship that, in
desperation to create a Jesus who conforms to *its*
view of what the Saviour should be, it has attempted
a presentation of Christianity which simply ignores or
eliminates large amounts of the Christian records. It
has thus proposed a radical reconstruction of the Old
and New Testament doctrine of the Kingdom, and then
attributed its own creation to Jesus!

10
Theology's Elimination of the Future Kingdom

The theological writings of our time are full of evidence to show how unfairly the teaching of Jesus about the Kingdom has been treated. Some of the most distinguished commentators seem to be determined to do away with the eschatological Kingdom of which Jesus spoke so habitually. Protests against such wholesale eradication of Jesus' teaching often appear only in footnotes. They deserve a much wider press.

For example, Leon Morris speaks of C. H. Dodd's 'realized eschatology' - the theory that the Kingdom had arrived with the ministry of Jesus and should not be looked for in the future - as "unsatisfactory to many." Unsatisfactory! It effectively wipes out the hope of the Kingdom to which the whole New Testament, indeed the whole Bible, strains. Leon Morris explains Professor Dodd's theory:

> "The eschaton (the end) has moved from the future to the present, from the sphere of expectation to that of realized experience."

According to Dodd there is no room in the teaching of Jesus for His real return. The reaction of the ordinary reader of the Bible will be one of horrified amazement that a professor of the New Testament could reach this conclusion. Morris goes on to say that that the theory of 'realized eschatology' "has been decisively rejected by many modern scholars." He quotes J. E. Fison as saying that "realized eschatology is frankly and flatly heretical by the standards of a considerable portion of the New Testament evidence." Emil Brunner is equally outspoken:

"It is clear that the future Coming is anything but a piece of mythology which can be
dispensed with. Whatever the form of the event
may be, the whole point lies in the fact that it
will happen. To try to boggle at it means to
boggle at the foundation of the faith, to smash
the cornerstone by which all coheres and apart
from which all falls to pieces. Faith in Jesus
Christ without the expectation of His Parousia
[Second Coming] is a voucher that is never
redeemed, a promise that is seriously meant. A
Christian faith without the expectation of the
Parousia is like a ladder that leads nowhere but
ends in a void" (*New International Commentary
on the New Testament*, I Thessalonians, p. 147). [20]

These are words brilliantly spoken and all too
true. The fact is that millions of church-goers have
no grasp at all of the future coming of Jesus to the
earth, much less of the reality of the Kingdom which
He has promised to inaugurate *on earth* at that time.
And yet the Kingdom of God and the Second Coming
which will introduce it are the centre and heart of
the Christian Gospel! In the absence of a clear exposition of the Kingdom, there clearly can be no authentic Christianity.

J. E. Fison's and Emil Brunner's insistence upon
the great future event is to be welcomed with
enthusiasm, but it is quite unsatisfactory to speak of
the Kingdom so vaguely—"Whatever the form of the
event may be"—when the New Testament and the Old
Testament in which it is rooted speak quite specifically. The restored theocracy is described in vivid detail
by the prophets. Sufficient is said in the New Testament to prove that the great Day of the Lord which,

---

[20] It is instructive to reflect on the alarming fact that a
distinguished New Testament scholar could have "smashed the
cornerstone" of New Testament faith. This may lead to further
consideration of what some "scholarship" is up to!

according to the Old Testament will introduce the Kingdom, is now associated with the return of Jesus in power and glory. A mass of material is found in the Old Testament describing world events which will precede and follow the Day of the Lord. A description of them must await a subsequent chapter.

We conclude our present discussion with a summary of its underlying thesis. Any claim that Jesus is the promised Messiah is incoherent unless the term "Messiah" is understood in its biblical context. There is no evidence in the New Testament that Jesus rejected any part of the role predicted for the Messiah in the Old Testament. He did not, however, *at His first coming*, seek to take up the messianic office as world ruler. It is a colossal mistake, however, to maintain that He *never* expected to govern the world as Messiah, the King, enthroned in Jerusalem. At His first coming He called and prepared His disciples for their part in the future Kingdom, and then submitted to death at the hands of the hostile Jewish and Roman officials. The Resurrection of Jesus which followed is the guarantee that He has overcome death and is therefore in a position one day to return to the earth to fulfil the remainder of the messianic mission and realize the prophets' vision of peace on earth. Meanwhile He continues at the right hand of the Father to administer His church, whom He invites to share in the messianic glory of the Coming Age. The failure of "theology" to do justice to this simple biblical scheme lies in its antipathy to things messianic (and thus to the Messiah Himself), and it has therefore lost sight of the central biblical fact that Jesus is the Messiah destined not only to die for the sins of mankind but to reign over the earth in a future theocracy initiated by His Second Coming. The primary task of churches, if they are to be the Church, is to proclaim that stupendous Good News.

PART II

Biblical Christianity's Messianic Framework And Its Disappearance From The Church

1
Salvation Through the Messiah

The Old and New Testament are thoroughly messianic documents. John Bright points out that the Messianic Kingdom is the unifying theme of scripture:

> "For the concept of the Kingdom of God involves, in a real sense, the total message of the Bible. Not only does it loom large in the teachings of Jesus, it is to be found, in one form or another, through the length and breadth of the Bible.... Old Testament and New Testament thus stand together as the two acts of a single drama. Act I points to its conclusion in Act II, and without it the play is an incomplete, unsatisfying thing. But Act II must be read in the light of Act I, else its meaning will be missed. For the play is organically one. The Bible is one book. Had we to give that book a title, we might with justice call it 'The Book of the Coming Kingdom of God'" (*Kingdom of God*, pp. 7, 197).

It is essential to remind ourselves that since Christ is only a translation of the Hebrew word for Messiah (= God's anointed King), the word 'Christianity' actually means 'Messianity.' Christians, in the biblical sense, are therefore 'Messianists,' followers of the Messiah. In view of these definitions it is a little disconcerting to find a leading New Testament scholar saying:

> "Today Messianism is dead, except for the sectarian fringe. Practically no one expresses his deepest convictions or hopes about the

universe in these categories.... No one seriously looks for a Messiah who will be the single solution to all the world's problems, spiritually or politically" (J. A. T. Robinson, *Human Face of God*, p. 9).

The point is that the New Testament, from beginning to end, *does* look for the solution to all the world's ills in a returning Messiah. [21]   For the New Testament Christians, the salvation effected by the death of Jesus did not complete the messianic drama. The world remained under the dominion and deception of Satan, who is its 'God' (II Cor. 4:4), and this awful situation will only be put right by the reappearance of the Messiah at the end of the age.   This is the authentic Christian outlook founded upon the prophets, the Apostles and Jesus Himself.

But if no one except in the sectarian fringe now expects a messianic resolution of our problems, it must be that the biblical Christian hope has been replaced by something else. If so, it is not surprising that contemporary church-goers find it difficult to relate sympathetically to much in Jesus' teaching. If they are strangers to things messianic—and Jesus is the Messiah—they will inevitably be strangers to Jesus, and He to them.

The New Testament presents Jesus' claim to Messiahship as the very heart of Christianity. All the titles conferred on Jesus by the New Testament stem directly from His claim to be the Messiah. Salvation, priesthood and kingship are the three basic ingredients of the office of Messiah. Moreover, the claim to be the Messiah is an exclusive claim. There can be only one genuine claimant and it is the purpose of biblical Christianity to show that Jesus, and Jesus alone, is the genuine Messiah. If we then ask how Jesus' authenticity is to be judged and assessed, the answer is simply that He fits the mould created for the

---

[21]   Our quotation may well prompt the question as to how far some scholarship is in sympathy with the New Testament.

Messiah by the Old Testament. The New Testament insists that Jesus has been able to do what the scriptures say the Messiah must, in the divine plan, accomplish. But the story is incomplete until the Messiah is installed as world ruler, restoring sound government to the earth. It is towards this messianic future that the New Testament strains in verse after verse. All is orientated towards the great coming crisis at which world power will change hands from Satan to Jesus.

An examination of the work of Paul and Peter in the book of Acts will show that they directed their efforts to demonstrating that Jesus was the promised King of Israel and Saviour of the world. Not only that, they made it clear that the resurrection of the Messiah and His present session with His Father form a prelude to the next great event in the divine programme of salvation: the return of Jesus to the earth. To the reasonable question as to why Jesus, if He is the Messiah destined to rule on David's throne, had now left the earth, Peter responds:

> *"Heaven must retain Jesus, the Messiah appointed for you, until the period of the Restoration of all things, about which times God spoke by the mouth of all His holy prophets from ancient time" (Acts 3:21).*

To Peter it is quite evident that the messianic programme is incomplete until the Restoration foreseen by all the prophets takes place. At that time God will send the Messiah (Acts 3:20). Until then "heaven must retain Him." Peter's outlook reflects the point of view of His Master who had promised the Apostles:

> *"In the New Age when the Son of Man will sit on His glorious throne, you also shall sit upon twelve thrones to rule the twelve tribes of Israel" (Matt. 19:28).*

The scheme underlying the New Testament is based

on a well known and remarkable portion of Psalm 110, which provided the subject matter of an interesting dialogue between Jesus and the Pharisees:

> *"Now while the Pharisees were gathered together, Jesus asked them a question saying, 'What do you think about the Messiah, whose Son is He?' They said to Him, 'The Son of David.' He said to them, 'How does David under inspiration call Him lord, saying, "The Lord said to my lord, sit at my right hand until I put thine enemies beneath thy feet." If David calls Him Lord, How is He his Son?'"* (Matt. 22:41-45).

The answer, of course, is that the Messiah was to be both David's descendant—his Son—and at the same time, paradoxically, his lord. The stinging point of Jesus' query was that David acknowledged Jesus as the Lord Messiah even before He had been born. The Pharisees, however, were unwilling to acknowledge that Jesus was the Messiah, though they could have known that He was a descendant of David, and had witnessed the miracles which accompanied His claims.

The progress of the messianic office is so concisely laid out by Psalm 110:1 that we find it quoted or alluded to some 25 times in the New Testament. It is the classic Old Testament revelation of the future of the Messiah and therefore indispensable for inculcating the framework of the faith. In two short lines it lays out the divine plan. The One God of Israel speaks to David's lord, the coming Messiah:

> *"The divine oracle of Yahweh to my lord [Messiah]: 'Sit at my right hand until I make your enemies your footstool.'"* [22]

---

[22] It is on the basis of this passage that we are to understand that Jesus has been declared "lord", i.e. "Lord Messiah" (see Acts 2:34-36). Peter here lays the foundation of New Testament Christology, defining Jesus' relationship to His Father. This apostolic statement about Jesus should not be dismissed as "Jewish," nor was it superseded by a more "advanced" view when John

This provides Peter with the information that:

> *"Heaven must receive the Messiah until the time of the Restoration of all things"* (Acts 3:21).

The anticipated subjection of the Messiah's enemies under His feet was the subject of another classic statement about the Messiah in the Psalms:

> *"As for me [Yahweh] I have installed my King [Messiah] upon Zion my holy mountain.... Ask of me and I will give you the nations as your inheritance and the very ends of the earth as your possession. You shall break them with a rod of iron. Thou shalt shatter them like earthenware"* (Psalm 2:6,8,9).

The story is both coherent and clear and was critically important for Jesus and the New Testament Church, who looked for the happy dénouement of the messianic drama at the return of Jesus. As we have seen, the risen Christ makes the promise of world rulership the spur for His disciples to remain faithful to the end:

> *"To him who overcomes and keeps my deeds to the end I will give authority over the nations"* (Rev. 2:26).

The resurrected Jesus repeats His promise under the New Covenant to confer royal office upon the Apostles. To them He had said at the last supper:

> *"Just as my Father has granted me a kingdom I grant you that you may eat and drink at*

---

wrote his gospel. John, like Peter, wrote with a single purpose in mind—to prove that Jesus was the Messiah, the Son of God (John 20:31). Post-biblical views of Jesus quickly disregarded these all-important facts and began to present a Jesus unlike Jesus, the Messiah. Gentile christology has an anti-semitic tendency; hence the loss of the Messianism of the New Testament and the consequent confusion over the Messiah's Kingdom.

my table in my kingdom, and you will sit on thrones administering the twelve tribes of Israel" (Luke 22:28-30).

Later in the Revelation the same privilege is extended to the church as a whole:

"He who overcomes I will grant to him to sit down with me on my throne as I also overcame and sat down with my Father on His throne" (Rev. 3:21).

In view of these promises of victory at the arrival of the Messiah to reign, it will not be difficult to understand the enthusiasm for the Messianic Kingdom expressed by the Apostles after they had completed six weeks of instruction about the Kingdom from the risen Jesus:

"He presented Himself alive, after His suffering, by many convincing proofs, appearing to them over a period of forty days and speaking of the things concerning the Kingdom of God....And so when they had come together, they were asking Him, saying, 'Lord, is it at this time you are restoring the kingdom to Israel?'" (Acts 1:3,6).

The question was, of course, the natural and proper one for anyone schooled by Jesus in the belief that He was the Messiah destined to establish the Kingdom of God. Jesus did nothing at all to shake their faith in the restoration of the Kingdom. When the great event would occur was, however, not to be revealed:

"It is not for you to know the times and seasons which the Father has fixed by His own authority" (Acts 1:7).

Jesus Himself had earlier confessed that He did not know the day or hour of His return (Mark 13:32). The question posed by the disciples in Acts 1:6

about the restoration of the Kingdom is proof positive of the messianic expectations instilled into them by their three and a half years' instruction in the company of Jesus, in addition to the forty days following the resurrection, during which Luke tells us they had been taught about "the things concerning the Kingdom of God" (Acts 1:3). It is in the commentaries on Acts 1:6 that the clash between biblical messianic Christianity and the traditional non-messianic version of the faith shows itself most obviously. The outlook of the Apostles is unmistakable. Their question about the restoration of the Kingdom to Israel showed that they fully expected the final establishment of the theocracy on earth. As the commentaries rightly state, this would mean the spiritual renovation of mankind "which had been the highest point of prophetic and apocalyptic expectation among the Jews" (*The Clarendon Bible*, Acts of the Apostles, p. 132). So it ought to be among the Christians.

This commentary goes on to say that the disciples' interest in the restoration of the Kingdom was "expressed in the language of the Old Jewish messianic hope." But that is hardly surprising! They used the language of the Jewish messianic hope because that was their hope! Jesus had done nothing whatever to undermine their Old Testament messianic expectation. His ministry had been concerned with the announcement of the Messianic Kingdom, the demonstration of its power, and the inculcation of the highest spiritual character in His disciples so that they might be found fit to take part in the Kingdom when it arrived. The "Jewish Messianic Kingdom," provided it was not divorced from the high ethical ideals required for participation in it, was none other than the hope of all the prophets, to which Jesus subscribed wholeheartedly. It is therefore misleading to speak of the disciples' hope for the restored Kingdom as 'Jewish' It is, in fact, Christian and Apostolic in the strictest sense. It is derived from Jesus Himself, who had come "to confirm the promises made to the Fathers" (Rom. 15:8).

Tragically, almost all commentators stumble at biblical Christianity at this critical verse in Acts 1:6. Since *they* have not appreciated the Gospel of the Kingdom of God, which was the core of Jesus' mission (Luke 4:43, etc.), they assume that the Apostles were wrong to think of the Kingdom in Jewish messianic terms. [23] They therefore find it necessary to attack the apostles (and by implication Jesus who had taught them extensively about the Kingdom) for hanging on to a Jewish understanding of the Kingdom. What they do not see is that this Jewish view of the Kingdom is the Old Testament one which Jesus endorsed. Certainly the Kingdom of God is not just a political event unconnected with a new spiritual dimension in the heart of man. Nor are we arguing that the Kingdom was not manifested in the ministry of Jesus; and indeed, the spiritual transformation which Christians undergo must, of course, happen now. But the stimulus for effort and endurance in the Christian race is the prospect of participation in the Messianic Kingdom of the future. This is the framework within which the whole New Testament scheme is built. For Jesus, unlike so many commentators who have misunderstood Him, there is nothing 'crude' or 'Jewish' about a new political order on earth with Messiah enthroned as King. That is the highest ideal revealed to man, and it is nothing less than the revealed purpose of God for humanity.

The constant tendency of expositors to condemn the disciples for their interest in the restored Kingdom illustrates traditional Christianity's antipathy to Jesus' Jewish messianic outlook. The problem is acute, for it affects the heart of the New Testament hope as well as the Gospel of the Kingdom. A completely

---

[23] A striking example of opposition to biblical Christianity is found in Calvin's commentary on this verse: "There are more mistakes in the Apostles' question than there are words." The real problem lies in Calvin's lack of sympathy with the Messianic Kingdom.

new orientation to the New Testament is required. Evidence for this will appear when commentators abandon their critical attitude to the Apostles in Acts 1:6 and share their vital interest in the Messianic Kingdom, which is the life blood of all that Jesus taught.

2
The Present Age and the Age to Come

The framework within which the New Testament is set is both Jewish and Messianic. A clearly defined world view is common to all the apostolic Christians, and the same view is shared by Jesus Himself. According to this view, the present system of things is thoroughly evil. Mankind is in the grip of evil cosmic forces from which it can be finally rescued only by the intervention of God Himself, who will send His Son the Messiah to defeat Satan and his demons. While it is possible for individual believers to be liberated from the tyranny of Satan even now, the whole world continues to "lie in the hands of the evil one" (I John 5:19), who "fools all the nations" (Rev. 12:9).

For Paul the era of history in which we are living until the arrival of the Messiah in glory is the "present evil age" (Gal. 1:4), dominated by Satan (II Cor. 4:4). The whole of creation is groaning while it awaits the revelation of the race of immortals to be 'born' at the resurrection (Rom. 8:23). It is true that Christians can already experience something of the salvation which will come to the world when Jesus sets up His Kingdom. They can even now be "transferred from the kingdom of darkness into the Kingdom of God" (Col. 1:13). But this must not mislead us into thinking that the Messianic Kingdom of God has actually arrived, for it cannot until the Messiah breaks through the clouds to take over the reins of world government. Until that glorious day the Christians are to pray "Thy Kingdom come," and, as Jesus tells us, it is when the cataclysmic events associated with the end of the age begin to occur that the faithful may know that "the Kingdom of God is about to come" (Luke 21:31, Good News Bible).

Both Jesus and the Apostles think of the present age as subject to Satan's dominion, and they look forward to the Coming Age of the manifested Kingdom of God consequent upon the Second Coming. It is this simple temporal framework which gives coherence to the New Testament. There is a well defined divine programme at work in the affairs of man and this enables the Christian to weather the storms of persecution and trial as he anticipates with exuberance the joys of the Coming Age of the Kingdom, when earth's ills will be made well and the faithful will receive the prize of immortality. Not only will the earth then be rescued from the curse of Satan, but the Christian who endures to the end will be granted an active part in the restoration of society under the messianic government which Jesus will inaugurate. In the New Testament there is a clearly defined goal to be reached at the Second Coming, and suffering, even to the point of martyrdom, can be cheerfully borne in view of the supreme reward which lies ahead.

The Christian objective is everywhere in the New Testament to gain "everlasting life"—or so our translations tell us. However, it is a commonplace of scholarship that the Greek expression in question actually means "Life in the Coming Age" [24] —that is, immortality and a place in the Age of the future Kingdom. By translating the Greek word 'aion' (age) by 'world,' the older translations helped to veil the typically Jewish contrast between "this age" and the "future age" of the Kingdom, which is fundamental to to biblical Christianity. [25] The two ages and the

---

[24] See, for example, C. K. Barratt, *The Gospel according to St. John:* "The meaning of 'the Life of Eternity' (Dan. 12:2) was expressed by the rabbis as 'the Life of the Coming Age'" (p. 179).

[25] See Matt. 12:32, Mark 10:30, Luke 16:8, Luke 18:30, Eph. 1:21, Heb. 6:5.

familiar Christian term "everlasting life," literally, "Life in the Coming Age," speak of the Messianism which is at the root of the whole New Testament.

3
Conflict in the Cosmos

As we have seen, Jesus traces the evil of our present system to a supremely wicked cosmic personality, Satan, the Devil. The Devil's activity, which permeates every facet of society, is furthered by a host of demonic forces who work in subtle and subversive ways to obscure the message of salvation, blinding the hearts of men and leading them away from the truth which could rescue them from Satan's deception.

The controlling influence of Satan is a fact of the universe as the writers of the New Testament understand it. And since Jesus is the Messiah who is destined to defeat Satan and his agents, it is obvious that He must carry on an unremitting struggle with the forces of evil. This the New Testament describes in detail, showing us the constant opposition with which Jesus was confronted in the form of demon, disease or hostile religious or political authorities. Looking back on the ministry of Jesus, John summarizes the Messiah's mission as a reversal of the works of the Devil: "The Son of God appeared for this purpose, that He might destroy the works of the devil" (I John 3:8). [26] It is the victory of the Messiah over the archenemy of mankind, won at the cost of his life. Yet it is a victory which is as yet far from complete, for John can still say that the world is totally in the grip of the evil one (I John 5:19). The good news is that "the god of this world," Satan (II Cor. 4:4), has

---

[26] Peter sums up the work of Jesus in exactly the same way: "God anointed Jesus of Nazareth who went about doing good, and healing all who were oppressed by the devil, for God was with Him" (Acts 10:38).

only a short time to carry on his nefarious work. The day of the Messiah will surely come when the Devil will be decisively put out of office (Rom. 16:20; Rev. 20:1-3). Then the Kingdom of God will prevail over all the earth.

This is the simple messianic story which underlies the whole of the New Testament records, each book contributing in its own individual way to a development of some aspect of the messianic drama. And drama it is indeed. For tension mounts as the world becomes more and more evil ("evil men shall grow worse and worse, deceiving and being deceived" — II Tim. 3:13), until finally the Messiah breaks in upon a careless and godless society and takes over the kingdoms of this world with irresistible power (Matt. 24:37-39; II Thess. 1:7,8): "The Lord Jesus shall be revealed from heaven with his mighty angels in flaming fire, dealing out retribution to those who do not know God and to those who do not obey the gospel of our Lord Jesus."

That these are the facts of the New Testament is really unarguable. The challenging question which arises, however, is why churches calling themselves Christian seem to operate in a totally different framework, having apparently discarded the New Testament world view with its characteristic philosophy of history and its burning hope for the reappearance of the Messiah at the end of the age. The question that must be faced is why it is fair to go on calling "Christian" a system of belief which seems to have dispensed with the fabric of what Jesus, the Christ, believed and taught.

4
Contemporary Theology's Anti-Messianic Tendency

Reading the works of contemporary 'liberal' theologians, one is struck by the cavalier fashion in which much of the New Testament's messianic themes are either ignored or disparaged. Referring to Jesus' question to the Pharisees about the Messiah, "What do you think about the Christ, whose Son is He?" J. A. T. Robinson points out that originally "it was a Jewish question expecting a Jewish answer," properly rendered by the NEB, "'What is your opinion about the Messiah?'" But this is not a Jewish question only. If it is asked by Jesus Christ, is it not by definition a Christian question, and if it was designed to teach the Pharisees a valuable lesson, ought it not likewise to instruct us Christians in what was closest to the heart of Jesus? Robinson thinks that 'Christ' is "severely conditioned historically and geographically. It is Jewish and late Jewish at that" (*The Human Face Of God*, pp. 1, 8). Yet the Christian writer to the Hebrews traces the messianic idea to the covenant made with David, assuming that his readers will know of the prophet Nathan's promise to David that his illustrious descendant will inherit the throne of his father (Heb. 1:5, Psalm 2:7, II Sam. 7:14). Psalm 110:1 is similarly a thoroughly messianic passage and is a constant favourite with the New Testament writers, since it so clearly and concisely outlines the messianic programme—the session of the Messiah with His Father now, as He awaits the moment for His return to inaugurate the Kingdom of God at the "restoration of all things" (Acts 2:34, 3:21). According to the New Testament writers, God had spoken of the Christ, whom they identify with Jesus, long before His birth in Bethlehem. Moses had directly predicted the birth of the Messiah when he wrote: "The Lord will raise up for you a prophet like me from among your country-men" (Deut. 18:15, cited in Acts 3:22, 7:37).

One of theology's most often used techniques for playing down the Messianism of the New Testament is the theory that the term 'Christ' "has taken on currency outside Judaism only by ceasing to be a title and becoming a proper name" (J. A. T. Robinson, *The Human Face of God*, p. 9). Now this may be all too tragically the case if one is referring to Christianity as it developed (or degenerated) *after the New Testament period*, but to maintain that in the New Testament, 'Christ' does not have its highly coloured official Jewish meaning is to undermine the whole thrust of apostolic Christianity—namely that Jesis is *the* Christ expected by the Jewish scriptures and that He acted, and is destined to act, accordingly.

Theologians even venture to tell us that 'Christ' was an appellation "with which Jesus Himself was unhappy" (ibid, p. 9), but this contradicts the obvious fact that Jesus saw recognition of Him as the Messiah as the great central revelation of the faith:

> *"He said to them, 'Who do you say that I am?' And Simon Peter said, 'Thou art the Christ, the Son of the living God.' And Jesus answered and said to him, 'Blessed are you, Simon Bar Jona, because flesh and blood did not reveal this to you but my Father who is in heaven'"* (Matt. 16:16, 17).

What Jesus went on to criticize in Peter was not the recognition that He was the Messiah (which was a blessed revelation from God!), but Peter's unwillingness to accept that it was through suffering and death that the Messiah's glory was to be reached.

Sometimes, it seems, scholars will try to direct our attention away from the title Messiah in order to convince us that Jesus preferred to be thought of as 'lord' or 'Son of God.'

> "As a theological category, to bear the weight and meaning the church saw in Jesus, 'Messiah,' with its political and eschatological overtones was soon superseded.... 'Christ' survived as a name interchangeable with 'Jesus'" (ibid. p. 9).

However, the political and eschatological associations of 'Messiah' are plainly evident in what the synoptic gospels record about Jesus. John's gospel has as its whole purpose the presentation of Jesus as the Messiah, King of Israel (John 20:21, 2:41,49). In the Revelation, the Jewish Messianism of Jesus, who speaks to the churches as Messiah in thoroughly messianic terms, is emphatically clear, as is the whole description, based on Old Testament prophecy, of His spectacular return in power to reign on the earth (5:10, 20:1-4, etc.).

We must recognize that Gentiles, who joined the ranks of the church in large numbers, did not easily grasp what it meant to believe in Jesus as Messiah. They were, however, ready to accept a God-figure of some kind. While the Apostles were alive, the admission of Gentiles into the church would not have been permitted without full instruction in the messianic teachings of Jesus. However, in post-apostolic times, there occurred a gradual loss of the meaning of the word 'Messiah' and thus the identity of the central figure of the faith became obscured and misunderstood.[27] It was this defection from the Messianism of

---

[27] Ridderbos notes that Paul's use of the term 'Christ' never loses its official flavour as the title of God's promised king: "However much the name Christ in the Pauline usage seems to have acquired the sense of a proper name, this does not mean that this designation has lost its official historic-Israelitic significance" (*Paul, An Outline of his Theology*, p. 51). The fact is that for us as Gentiles 'Christ' may seem to be a proper name. But in order to understand the New Testament, we must learn that 'Christ' is a title which belongs to the promised Son of David, who is destined to set up His world-wide rule in the Coming Age. The Messianic flavour of the New Testament can be recaptured if one reads the word 'Messiah' in place of the word 'Christ.'

Jesus which spelled the demise of biblical Christianity, and it accounts for the strangeness of the messianic concept to those who have not been schooled in the Christianity of the Bible. It is quite unfair, however, to attribute a loss of the Messiahship of Jesus to the New Testament Christians, for whom the understanding of Jesus as the one and only Messiah was the great central confession of the faith. Any loss of this heart of the creed was viewed as anti-Christian:

> *"Whoever believes that Jesus is the Messiah is born of God" (I John 5:1).*
> *"Who is the liar but the one who denies that Jesus is the Messiah. This is the antichrist..." (I John 2:22).*

It is clear that belief in Jesus as the promised Messiah formed the basis of the whole apostolic mission. It is the unifying theme of the whole New Testament. To admit, then, that Gentiles were allowed to become members of the church without understanding the Messiahship of Jesus is simply to confess that the church lost its grip on the whole original point of Christianity's central figure. [28]

When theologians now tell us that 'Christ' became only a meaningless surname and lost its official Hebrew meaning, they are describing a *loss* of the original faith, not a legitimate development of it. The fact is that most theologians are also not much taken with a Jesus who is the Messiah of Israel, and they therefore report without much sadness that "Messianism is dead except for the sectarian fringe."

---

[28] J. Y. Campbell in *A Theological Word Book of the New Testament*, ed. Alan Richardson, p. 46, says: "In Christian usage 'Christ' first acquired a new and different meaning and then lost all meaning and became simply a name like 'Jesus' itself." He admits, however, that Jesus could not have been understood if He had given 'Messiah' an entirely new meaning. Our point is simply that the loss of the meaning of the word 'Messiah' meant a loss of the identity of Jesus. This made way for the substitution of an unmessianic saviour who is alien to the New Testament.

This may only be another way of saying that New Testament Christianity is dead except in the minds of the minority, who still trust in Jesus as the Messiah of Old Testament prophecy and the King of the Messianic Kingdom, which still awaits its inauguration on the earth when the Messiah comes to rule. For that minority it would be hard to know what is meant by the petition "thy Kingdom come" if it were not a cry for the establishment of the messianic government worldwide, and thus for the return of Jesus.

Since, as is widely admitted, the Kingdom of God is the controlling idea of all Jesus' teaching, we can appreciate how fatal would be the loss of the messianic ideas associated with the Kingdom. It would inevitably lead to a reinterpretation of Jesus' teaching which strips it of its messianic character. Can, however, such a reinterpretation really be anything other than a rewriting of Christianity in non-messianic terms? And how could this avoid the nonsensical contradiction involved in divorcing the Messiah from His messianic teaching? Would a Christianity emptied of its essential messianic characteristics still amount to a faith recognizably apostolic?

5
The Influence of Gnosticism

The cause of the radical shift away from belief in Jesus as Messiah, in the fully biblical sense of the word, is not hard to detect. It was the influence of gnosticism which "spoke of something universal in man, and was indeed the first factor in lifting 'the Christ' out of the narrow confines of Jewish Messianism" (*The Human Face of God*, p. 7). It was against the threat of gnosticism that the Apostles battled continuously as they sought to preserve the Jewish messianic framework in which biblical Christianity is set.[29] The first target of the gnostics was the resurrection of the dead, which for the Apostles meant the calling to life of the faithful dead to gain immortality. It was the great event associated with the return of the Messiah to set up His Kingdom.

> *"In Christ all shall be made alive. But each in his own order: Christ the firstfruits, after that, those who are Christ's **at his coming"** (I Corinthians 15:22, 23).*

The struggle to preserve the pure New Testament doctrine of the resurrection was unfortunately lost in the centuries following the death of the Apostles. Though certainly the church claimed that it was winning the battle, what actually happened was a partial surrender to the gnostics. What survived as 'Christian' teaching about life after death owes as much to gnosticism as it does to the teaching of Jesus and the Apostles. According to the New Testament the dead are at present 'asleep' in the

---

[29] See, for example, I Tim. 6:20, II Tim. 2:18, I Cor. 15:12: "Why do some of you say there is no resurrection from the dead?"

grave waiting to be called into life again when Jesus returns.[30]   It is then that "all those who are in the tombs shall hear His voice, and shall come forth, those who did good to a resurrection of life..." (John 5:28, 29). The simple picture of the dead returning to life through resurrection is based on the Hebrew understanding of man as a psychosomatic unit. The whole man dies and the whole man comes to life again. Thus the prediction of resurrection in Daniel 12:2 declares that "many who are sleeping in the dust of the ground shall awake, some to everlasting life" ("everlasting life" meaning literally, "Life in the Coming Age of the Kingdom").

What goes by the name of resurrection in most of the churches is something rather different, bearing the marks of the gnostic infiltration into the original faith. Popular belief, sustained by funeral sermons and indoctrination from early childhood, sees the dead as already fully alive in heaven as disembodied souls, an idea which, as so many competent scholars have pointed out, would be both repugnant and unintelligible to the Hebrew writers of the New Testament.[31] (Luke, the only Gentile author, was thoroughly steeped in Hebraic ways of thinking.) The aim of the traditional teaching is, no doubt, to comfort the bereaved with

---

[30]   It is interesting to note the warning sounded by Justin Martyr about 150.A.D.: "For if you have fallen in with some who are called Christian, but who do not admit the truth of the resurrection and venture to blaspheme the God of Abraham, Isaac and Jacob; who say that there is no resurrection of the dead but that their souls when they die are taken to heaven: Do not imagine that they are Christians" (*Dialogue with Trypho*, ch. 80).

[31]   Cp. the remarks of the British theologian, Alan Richardson, D.D.: "The Bible writers, holding fast to the conviction that the created order owes its existence to the wisdom and the love of God and is therefore essentially good could not conceive of life after death as a disembodied existence ('We shall not be found naked' — II Cor. 5:3) but as a renewal under new conditions of the intimate unity of body and soul which was human life as they knew it. Hence death was thought of as *the death of the whole man* ..." (*A Theological Word Book of the Bible*, p. 111, emphasis added).

the belief that the departed are not really dead, but it has had the devastating effect of relegating the future resurrection of the dead (as well as the whole New Testament scheme of the future) to a redundant appendage tagged on to the end of the creed. For, as William Tyndale argued with the Roman Catholic Church, what point is there in a future resurrection of the dead if in fact they have already achieved their glory in heaven? And, we must add, what need for a Messianic Kingdom on earth when the Messiah returns? Once the Christian objective is shifted from its biblical focal point at the return of Jesus to reign, a loss of New Testament perspective is inevitable. It will not be hard to see why the New Testament scheme for the future makes so little impact on church goers. It simply will not fit with what they have been taught to think of as Christian teaching about life after death. A return to biblical Christianity will mean the reinstating of the pillar of Christian hope for the future—the resurrection of the *dead* (not just dead bodies) at the Coming of Jesus. Those who preside at funeral services should consider the observations of J. A. T. Robinson:

> "The whole of our Western tradition has contrived to give death an altogether inflated significance. There has been a vastly exaggerated focus on death and the moment of death. It began when the pages of the New Testament were hardly dry, and it is one of the most remarkable silent revolutions in the history of Christian thought.... The whole of our teaching and our hymnology has assumed that you go to heaven—or, of course, hell—when you die.... This proposition is in clear contradiction with what the Bible says.... The Bible nowhere says that we go to heaven when we die, nor does it ever describe death in terms of going to heaven.... Wesley's words 'Bid Jordan's narrow stream divide, and bring us safe to heaven' have no

biblical basis" (*On Being the Church in the World*, pp. 129, 130, 131).

The recovery of apostolic Christianity will be thwarted as long as preachers and teachers fail to recognize the gulf which separates our view of the future from that of the Apostles. New Testament Christianity is set within a framework which tradition has dismantled. Rebuilding the New Testament framework begins with a restoration of the Second Advent and the ensuing Kingdom of God on earth as the focal point of all our Christian thinking. Without this clear vision of the Kingdom (which is the vision of all the prophets, as is well known), we cannot respond intelligently to what Jesus and the Apostles taught.

The task of evangelical theology must be to eliminate the pagan Greek philosophical element which has usurped the place of the original Hebraic teaching of the Bible. We must define the Kingdom of God as Jesus and the prophets defined it, and abandon our natural Gentile aversion to the messianic hope of future peace on earth with the arrival of the Messiah in glory.

6
Demythologizing

The prospect of abandoning tradition and returning to the simple teachings of the early church ought to be an inviting one. There is a thrill to be experienced in rediscovery and a sense of common identity with the early followers of the Messiah. So far, however, theology has been trying to lead us in a different direction. What we need to do, it has been argued, is remove from the New Testament those aspects of its teaching which will not fit with our modern scientific view of the world. More specifically, the 'myths' of the New Testament such as the Virgin Birth, Miracles, the literal resurrection of Jesus and the Second Coming should be so reinterpreted in modern terms that they will not prove offensive to the scientifically sensitive.

The extent of the 'demythologising' process will vary from one writer to another, but common to all is the conviction that we simply cannot accept what Jesus and the early church believed. Almost certainly miracles will have to go, or at least many of them. The remainder can be explained 'psychologically.' The resurrection, as the real reappearance of Jesus after His death, and the empty tomb will have to be questioned in order to see if a 'simpler' explanation can be found. As for the Virgin Birth, that is only a way of speaking about the uniqueness of Jesus. It must not be taken as a biologically accurate account of the facts, nor should the Second Coming be thought of as a real event of the future.

It is surprising that anyone could imagine that what survives this sophisticated attack on the Christian documents is recognizably Christian, when the pillars of the New Testament faith have been removed. Perhaps it is, as Oscar Wilde said cynically, that "truth in matters of religion is simply the opinion that survives." Truth, in reality, is what Jesus and the Apostles believed and taught.

7
Evangelicalism's Gospel Without the Kingdom

The evangelical part of the church-going public has seen that to abandon Scripture as an authoritative and final source of the Christian faith is to open the doors to religious anarchy. However, evangelicals unwittingly accept as biblical truth a great deal that has not been carefully examined in the light of Scripture. The 'Sola Scriptura' slogan of the Reformation may often mean only a *traditional* explanation of the Scriptures.

This is significantly true of the evangelical definition of the Gospel.[32] Once again it is the Messianism of the New Testament which has been abandoned. The Gospel which Jesus and the Apostles proclaimed was always the *Gospel of the Kingdom of God* (Matt. 4:23, 24:14, Luke 4:43, Acts 8:12, 28:23, 31). The enormously important and almost entirely overlooked Lukan formula describing the Gospel states that belief in the Kingdom of God and the things concerning Jesus is necessary before baptism (Acts 8:12, 28:23, 31). It was the preaching of that Gospel which Jesus saw as the whole raison d'être of His mission (Luke 4:43). But the failure of traditional Christianity to define the Kingdom in biblical messianic terms has led to the substitution of a partial "believe in Jesus" Gospel. The

---

[32] Appeal is usually made to 1 Cor. 15:1-4 without mention of the complementary evidence of Acts 8:12, 28:23,31, 19:8, 20:25, which show that the Kingdom of God was always the centre of the apostolic Gospel. In 1 Cor. 15:1-3 Paul is concerned with the vital information about the death and resurrection of Jesus which he had preached "amongst things of first importance" (v. 3).

Kingdom seems to have disappeared from the Good News. The problem is that the Gospel deprived of its strong eschatological and messianic associations is not really the Gospel as Jesus and the Apostles preached it. There is a clear difference between the traditional "departing to heaven when you die" and the New Testament expectation of resurrection to life in the Kingdom at the Second Coming. In the New Testament the Good News about the Kingdom of God is first put to the potential convert (Mark 1:15,16); "Repent and believe the Good News" (about the Kingdom of God). With this message he is challenged by a statement about God's purpose for the future of our world. God plans to send His Son to establish the Kingdom of God on earth. He has already sent Him to announce that Good News and exercise the power of the Kingdom in healing and exorcism. Jesus has been temporarily transferred to the presence of His Father to act as High Priest for the Church.

All of us are sinners in need of forgiveness and redemption. God's Son, the Messiah, the prophesied Suffering Servant of Isaiah 53, died for our sins. In Him we may find forgiveness. Initiation into the Christian community is by baptism, once the essential facts of the "Gospel of the Kingdom and the things concerning the name of Jesus" have been grasped (Acts 8:12, 28:23, 31). Following baptism as evidence of our commitment to God and His Son, we should spend the remainder of our lives "growing in grace and knowledge,"[33] in preparation for the great event of the future, the ushering in of a new order of things.

In the New Testament Gospel, the Second Coming and the ensuing Kingdom are at the heart of the message, *in addition to* the central fact of the death and resurrection of the Messiah. Not only is the Kingdom placed before the potential convert with a challenge to believe in the Good News (Mark 1:14, 15), but the would-be disciple is invited to prepare himself for

---

[33]   II Pet. 3:18

an active executive part in the restoration of peace on earth when the Messiah comes to reign. At once an objective is established which gives coherence to the whole Christian venture:

> *"Behold, we have left everything and followed you. What then will there be for us? And Jesus said to them, 'Truly I say to you, you who have followed me, in the Regeneration, when the Son of Man will sit on His glorious throne, you also shall sit upon twelve thrones to govern the twelve tribes of Israel'"* (Matt. 19:27, 28).

> *"When the Son of Man comes, then He will sit on his glorious throne..."* (Matt. 25:31).

> *"You are those who have stood by me in my trials, and just as my Father has granted me a kingdom, I grant you that you may eat and drink at my table in my kingdom, and you will sit on thrones to govern the twelve tribes of Israel"* (Luke 22:28-30).

> *"Fear not little flock for it is your Father's good pleasure to give you the kingdom"* (Luke 12:32).

> *"When he returned after receiving the kingdom, he said to him, 'Well done, good slave, because you have been faithful in a very little thing, be in authority over ten cities'"* (Luke 19:15, 17).

> *"Do you not know that the saints will govern the world.... Do you not know that the unrighteous shall not inherit the Kingdom of God?"* (I Cor. 6:2, 9).

> *"If we endure, we shall also reign with Him"* (II Tim. 2:12).

> *"He who overcomes I will grant him to sit down with me on my throne as I also overcame and sat down with my Father on His throne"* (Rev. 3:21).

> *"Thou hast made them to be a kingdom of*

priests to our God and they shall reign on the earth" (Rev. 5:10).

"They came to life and reigned with the Messiah for a thousand years" (Rev. 20:4).

Most of this emphasis on the future kingdom and the believer's part in it is missing from evangelism in our time. The significant difference separating New Testament presentations of the Gospel from contemporary ones is demonstrated by the candid acknowledgement by leading evangelicals (cited earlier) that they are puzzled by the total absence of the word 'kingdom' in their discussions and preaching of the Gospel. This is because they have been trapped by a gentilized version of the faith, which is essentially unmessianic and has lost its grip on the Good News about the Kingdom of God.

Evangelicals may be surprised at the suggestion that their gospel is not fully based on the Bible. They may turn to I Cor. 15:1-3 to show that Paul's three-point summary of the Gospel consisted in the death, burial and resurrection of Jesus. This is true, as far as it goes, but they have not noted carefully that Paul preached these facts "amongst things of first importance" (I Cor. 15:3). It was not *all* that Paul preached as the Gospel, for the Book of Acts insists that Paul preached "the Kingdom of God and the things concerning Jesus" (Acts 28:23, 31) and, as these verses show, this message was proclaimed to Jew and Gentile alike as the message of salvation. Precisely the same formula describes the preaching of Philip in Acts 8:12:

"When they believed Philip as he proclaimed the Good News about the Kingdom of God and the name of Jesus, they were baptized, both men and women."

Clearly the Kingdom of God was the *first* item on the agenda in apostolic presentations of the Gospel. This is hardly surprising, since Jesus had always proclaimed the Gospel of the Kingdom—and this was long before anything at all was said about His death for our sins, which the disciples did not yet understand! (Luke 18:31-34)! It is immensely instructive to note that the subject matter of the Kingdom cannot originally have included the death and resurrection of Jesus. The Apostles had proclaimed the Gospel of the Kingdom before they knew anything about the cross. This is why Luke in Acts is careful to tell us that the apostolic proclamation *after the resurrection* maintained its primary emphasis on the Kingdom of God, and *added* the new information about the death of Jesus as "the things concerning His name" (Acts 8:12, 28:23, 31). It is crucially important to observe that Paul could describe his whole ministry as "the preaching of the Kingdom" (Acts 20:25), just as Jesus had seen the Gospel of the Kingdom as the raison d'être of His mission (Luke 4:43). But could contemporary evangelicals demonstrate their faithfulness to apostolic practice when, at an international conference on evangelism, they admit that the Kingdom of God "is not our language" (Michael Green, at the Lausanne Convention on Evangelism, 1974)? If the Kingdom is not their language, they are not preaching the Gospel!

The absence of the Kingdom from contemporary statements of the Gospel is a serious defect which can only be rectified by rediscovering the messianic message of God's future reign on earth in the persons of the Messiah and His followers. Not only the Kingdom, but the Messiahship of Jesus must be put back into the centre of the Christian proclamation. The confession of Peter at Caesarea Philippi must not be allowed to suffer the slightest alteration, for it is the rock foundation of the faith, nor must the title 'Son of God' be removed from its biblical context, lest it take on an unbiblical meaning. In Scripture it is plainly and simply an extension of the messianic title based on Psalm 2:7 and the Davidic covenant in II Sam. 7:14. To invest someone with the title 'Son of God' in the Bible is equivalent to hailing Him as Messiah, a unique and specially anointed representative of God. Evangelicals must close the gap that appeared in post-biblical times between the two titles, Christ and Son of God, under the influence of unmessianic Christianity. A stimulus to a return to the right understanding of the Son of God is given in Luke 1:35: The Son of God comes into being miraculously in Mary's womb.

It has been most wisely said that "to worship Christ with the wrong beliefs about Him is to worship a false Christ, by whatever name we call Him; for we, in so doing, falsely imagine him to be other than He is and other than He is revealed in Scripture to be" (R. A. Cole, *Tyndale N. T. Commentary on Mark*, pp. 199). It must be clear that a Gospel deprived of its central theme, the Kingdom (as it obviously is in contemporary evangelism), and a Jesus who is not perfectly matched with the Messiah of Scripture, both as to His identity and His role, threaten the whole fabric of the New Testament faith. Received systems of belief and preaching must therefore be subjected to critical scrutiny by those seeking to worship God, through His Son, the Messiah, in spirit and in truth (John 4:24).

8
Accommodation to Mystery Religion

Historians tell us that there are striking points of similarity between Christianity and pagan mystery cults.

"For one thing all of them had some form of initiation ceremony. In the case of Mithraism this was exactly the same as Christianity, namely baptism" (*Is Christianity True?* Michael Arnheim, p. 127).

In the cult of Attis, a young lover of Cybele, there was a celebration of the death of the saviour (Attis) and of his resurrection three days later. These are not the only points of contact between the pagan and the traditional Christian calendars:

"If Easter owes much to Cybele, Christmas is largely derived from Mithras (plus the old Roman festival of the Saturnalia, a jolly occasion on which gifts were exchanged). Mithras, associated as he was with the sun, gave Christianity December 25th as the date for Christians.... What is more, Mithras, like Jesus, was believed to have had a miraculous birth and to have attracted, as an infant, the attention of the neighbouring shepherds. In addition, Mithraism, like Christianity, had a sacramental meal as part of its ceremonial. But perhaps the most important element common to Christianity and the pagan mystery cults was the concept of salvation. In one sense or another, Isis, Cybele, and Mithras were all seen as saviours. . ." (ibid. p. 27).

It is not hard to see how Christianity and the mystery cults could have become confused in the minds of improperly instructed Gentile believers. The tendency to reinterpret the Messiah in Gentile terms and the tell-tale signs of gnosticism in traditional Christianity suggest that a significant accommodation to paganism has taken place. The opinion of one widely recognized Lutheran scholar should be carefully noted:

> "The hope of the early church centred on the resurrection of the Last Day. It is this which *first* calls the dead into eternal life (I Cor. 15, Phil. 3:20ff). This resurrection *happens to the man and not only to the body.* Paul speaks of the resurrection not 'of the body' but 'of the dead.' This understanding of the resurrection implicitly understands *death as also affecting the whole man.... Thus the original biblical concepts have been replaced by ideas from Hellenistic gnostic dualism.* The New Testament idea of the resurrection which affects *the whole man* has had to give way to the immortality of the soul. The Last Day also loses its significance, for souls have received all that is decisively important long before this. Eschatological tension is no longer strongly directed to the day of Jesus' Coming. The difference between this and the hope of the New Testament is very great" (Dr. Paul Althaus, *The Theology of Martin Luther*, pp. 413, 414, emphasis mine).

Norman H. Snaith, M.A., D.D. (Oxon) makes a significant contribution to our discussion. He sounds a warning note that all is not well with 'official' Christianity when he says:

> "The whole Bible, the New Testament as well as the Old Testament, is based on the Hebrew attitude and approach. We are of the firm opinion that this ought to be recognized on all hands to a greater extent. It is clear to

us...that there is often *a great difference between Christian theology and biblical theology*. Throughout the centuries the Bible has
been interpreted in a Greek context, and even
the New Testament has been interpreted on the
basis of Plato and Aristotle.... Our position is
that the reinterpretation of biblical theology in
terms of the ideas of Greek philosophers has
been both widespread throughout the centuries
and everywhere destructive to the essence of
the Christian faith.... If these judgments are
sound, and we believe that they are sound, then
*neither Catholic nor Protestant theology is
based on biblical theology.* In each case we
have a domination of Christian theology by
Greek thought" (*The Distinctive Ideas of the
Old Testament*, pp. 185, 187, 188, emphasis added).

In addition, the whole vexed question now being so
widely discussed about the relation of Jesus to the
One God of the strict biblical monotheism needs to be
examined by seekers after the purity of apostolic
faith. It is remarkable that for Paul (as for Jesus)
there was no theoretical difficulty for monotheism
about Jesus being the Son of God, the Messiah. Only
when a subtly different claim that He was "God the
Son" was introduced did the whole Trinitarian question
arise. The current illuminating discussion about the
presence or absence of the developed doctrine of the
incarnation of the second member of a Triune God in
scripture should be carefully investigated by evangelicals before they jump to hasty conclusions about the
biblical basis of traditional creeds. (See, for example,
Christology in the Making, by James Dunn, and *The
Human Face of God*, by J. A. T. Robinson, especially
chapter 5, *God is Spirit*, by Geoffrey Lampe, chapter 5, and especially *The Christian Experience of God
as Trinity*, by James P. Mackey, chapter 6: "The
Problem of the Pre-existence of the Son."

For those not wishing to tackle the subject in so

much detail, it will be sufficient to examine the
illuminating creed of Jesus recorded in Mark 12:28-34
as well as Paul's classic credal statement about what
Christians believe in I Cor. 8:4-6. His definition of
the One God as distinct from Jesus, the one Lord
Messiah, should be noted carefully:

> "There is no God but one. For even if
> there be so-called gods in heaven and on
> earth (as indeed there are many gods and many
> lords), yet for us there is but one God, the
> Father, and one Lord Jesus Messiah...."

At the close of his ministry Paul again states the
apostolic creed:

> "There is one God, and one mediator be-
> tween God and man, the man Messiah Jesus"
> (I Tim. 2:5).

These revealing verses show that Paul never for
an instant abandoned the strict monotheism of the
Jewish heritage he shared with Jesus. The One God
of Christian monotheism is the *Father*. This is uni-
tary, not Trinitarian monotheism, as so many contemporary scholars recognize; and John is as undeviating a
witness to this form of monotheism as any New
Testament writer (John 5:44, 17:3). His one purpose is
to make us believe in Jesus as *Messiah* (John 20:31).

9
A Call for a Return to New Testament Christianity

The New Testament presents us with an essentially simple doctrine of the church. It is the continuation of the faithful congregation of Israel, now composed of Jew and Gentile, and enjoying equal status as part of the spiritual "Israel of God" (Gal. 6:16). The citizens of this community are to be, in the words of Jesus, *"not part of this world"* (John 15:19). They are to be separate and different from the world as ambassadors of the Kingdom of God (II Cor. 5:20) and thus manifest the holiness of the God who inspires them through His spirit.

One of the most perplexing and troubling aspects of traditional Christianity is its failure to put into practice the ideals of conduct demanded by Jesus of His followers. These are laid out with particular clarity in the Sermon on the Mount, where the requirements of discipleship are taught. Christians are commanded to love their opponents and not to resist evil persons. In so doing they are to conform to a new standard: that of loving their enemies (Matt. 5:38-48). In the past, Jesus pointed out, it was customary to hate the national enemies of Israel (it had never been permissible to hate a fellow Israelite enemy). Under the Christian ethic, however, enemies of all sorts are to be loved and not resisted. The incompatibility of this teaching with participation in the war machine is obvious. Even the traditional just war theory, if it could be reconciled with Scripture, is utterly inadequate under modern conditions where nuclear weapons threaten the lives of combatants and non-combatants alike.

Moreover, the whole body of Christians is to be recognized by the world as disciples of Jesus by the love which unites them:

"By this shall all men recognize you, if you have love one for another" (John 13:35).

In this community bonded by love, there is to be "no distinction between Greek and Jew, circumcised and uncircumcised, barbarian, Scythian, slave and freeman" (Col. 3:11) and, we might add, "American, Russian and French Christian," but Christ is all in all. The first obvious implication of this teaching is that Christians cannot possibly be involved in the slaughter of their brethren in other lands, and it is therefore imperative for them to separate themselves from the use of violence which inevitably renders them guilty of the blood of their fellow Christians in other nations, as well as their enemies. It really is outrageous that Christians can think that they can go on contemplating the mass destruction of their spiritual brethren, as for example happened in the last war when countless Lutheran Christians in Germany and British Christians in England took each other's lives. [34] The only possible course consistent with Jesus' instructions is to "come out and be separate" and maintain the bond of love by which "all men shall recognize you as my disciples." In maintaining the New Testament example of

---

[34] One who saw the inconsistency of Christians taking each other's lives was an Archdeacon in the Church of England: "Within the Christian fellowship each is to be linked to each other by a love like that of Christ for each. That is the new commandment; and obedience to it is to be evidence to the world of true discipleship....Such is the quality of love designed for the unity of His Church. But can anything conflict more completely with such an ideal than that Christians should go to war against Christians?....Can anyone outside a madhouse suggest that when, for example, British and American Christians accepted responsibility for dropping the atomic bomb which killed and maimed in body and soul their fellow-Christians in Nagasaki, such an act could be 'evidence' to the world that within the Christian fellowship they were linked by a love like that of Christ for each other?" (Percy Harthill, *The Church*, p. 49).

separation from the state, Christians will be true to their status as ambassadors resident in a 'foreign' and hostile world, and they will witness as a colony of the Kingdom of God to the world-wide peace which will come to the earth when Jesus returns to reign.

10
Tradition —
The Great Barrier to Progress

The difficulty in gaining acceptance for what we are proposing lies not in the complexity of the subjects under discussion but in the tenacity with which "the way we have always believed" grips the minds of sincere church-goers. Biblical Christianity, which cannot flourish unless it is accepted with the mind "of a little child," is nothing more than belief in, and surrender to, the Father as "the only true God" (John 17:3), and to Jesus as Messiah, who died for the sins of the world and is now High Priest over His people drawn from every nation. He will return to gather his followers into the Kingdom to be inaugurated on the earth. It is the long-standing "demessianized" version of the faith, widely and uncritically accepted, which makes it hard for us to relinquish cherished understandings. But for evangelicals especially there should be a great appeal in the challenge to return to the Bible and begin to proclaim, first and foremost, "the Gospel of the *Kingdom* and the things concerning the Name of Jesus" (Acts 8:12, 28:23, 31).

The thesis underlying this challenge to surrender unconditionally to the apostolic teachings of the Bible is that church-goers have unwittingly taken on board a great measure of post-biblical Greek theology which is foreign to and incompatible with what the Apostles taught. This complaint is certainly not original, but it has so far not gained a wide hearing. A celebrated Oxford scholar wrote in 1889:

"I venture to claim to have shown that a large part of what are sometimes called

Christian doctrines, and many usages which have prevailed and continue to prevail in the Christian church are in reality Greek theories and Greek usages changed in form and colour by the influence of primitive Christianity, but in their essence Greek still. ... The question which forces itself upon our attention as the phenomena pass before us in review is the question of the relation of these Greek elements to the nature of Christianity itself. The question is vital; its importance can hardly be overestimated" (Edwin Hatch, *The Influence of Greek Ideas on Christianity*, pp. 350-1).

If, as we have contended, the Greek mind has distorted our understanding of the meaning of 'Christ' and of His Gospel of the Kingdom, nothing could exceed in importance the need for a thorough reexamination, at the personal, family and church levels, of these central building blocks of the faith. As a stimulus to weeding out from our belief systems what is not genuinely Christian, we should remember also the warning of a British theologian who wrote:

"When the Greek mind and the Roman mind in turn, instead of the Hebrew mind, came to dominate the church's outlook, there occurred a disaster from which we have never recovered, either in practice or in doctrine. If today a great age of evangelization is to dawn, we need the Jews again" (Canon H. Goudge in *Collected Essays on Judaism and Christianity*).

Quite specifically, we need the Jew Jesus, the Messiah of Israel and Saviour of the world who, we suspect, has been overshadowed or even replaced by a Gentile 'Jesus.'

The same point is made by Olga Levertoff:

"The Church must retrace her steps to find again the prophetic spirit of the revolutionary leaders of ancient Israel. She must be prepared to break with much that time has hallowed or privilege made dear. 'Back to the first-century church' must be her slogan - which practically means back to Jewish Christianity" (*The Jews in a Christian Social Order*).

This does not, of course, mean back to Judaism, but to the genuine Christianity of Jesus and Paul, a Christianity centred in belief in Jesus as the Lord Messiah of Hebrew expectation, and in the Messianic Kingdom which He and His followers with Him will administer on earth when He comes again.

Throughout the New Testament it is assumed that Christians will become familiar with the Old Testament, especially the message and predictions of the prophets, and that its authority as well as that of Jesus and the Apostles will be unquestioned. The widespread defection from this Christian perspective is rapidly leading to spiritual anarchy.

Though the New Testament is written in the Greek language, its controlling ideas are Hebrew, derived from the Old Testament, and its grand central theme is the Good News about the Kingdom of God to be realized through the work of Jesus, the promised Messiah. Unless these principles are basic to a system of theology, that theology can make no claim to be apostolic. Once the Kingdom of God is 'reinterpreted' in terms of "the social gospel," or merely a kingdom "in the heart," and its apocalyptic association with a future crisis in history is discarded, we have no right to identify it with the teaching of Jesus and the Apostles. In other words, unless the Second Coming of Jesus and subsequent Kingdom on earth remain as central as His resurrection in Christian thinking, we must admit to a loss of an essential element of the messianic programme. The hope for the return of Messiah in history to renew the world must be reinstated and maintained against all the varied and essentially gnostic efforts to remove it or empty it of its biblical meaning. As is well known, every imaginable device has been employed by theologians to eliminate the Second Coming and the Kingdom which follows. It has been dismissed as 'poetry,' or the texts which describe it in detail are dissolved into thin air with protests that they cannot be taken literally. This is a form of theological cowardice. It is time to stop retreating from the messianic sayings of Jesus and embrace them, thankful for the hope they offer for peace on earth.

Evasive treatment of plain language amounts only to refusal to "hear the word of God." We dare not rewrite the Christian faith to suit ourselves. What stands written as "the faith once and for all delivered to the saints" contains the record not only of the unique birth of the Messiah and His return to life after death, but also the promise of our resurrection destined to occur when Jesus returns to inaugurate a new era of history from which Satan will be banished. Could anything be more relevant to our sin-sick world? And what greater and yet more humbling privilege could be conceived than for Christians to have a part in the reorganization of mankind in the New Society of the coming Kingdom of God on earth?

11
Prediction in the New Testament

No aspect of the New Testament has suffered more at the hands of criticism than that which deals with predictions about the future. The confusion and conflict which have resulted are to be found in standard commentaries. In Mattew 24 (parallel to Mark 13 and Luke 21) Jesus gave an essentially straightforward account of events which will lead up to His return to inaugurate the Kingdom. It is an account, as Jesus says, grounded in the predictive revelations granted to Daniel, and it is a coherent description of the final stages of the present evil age, just before Jesus' reappearance. Evidently Jesus believed that the book of Daniel contained information about the distant future, and He therefore instructed His followers to consult the words of Daniel in order to grasp the meaning of His own view of the future (Matt. 24:15):

> *"When you see the Desolating Horror*
> *spoken of through Daniel the prophet,*
> *standing in the holy place (let the reader*
> *understand), then let those who are in Judea*
> *flee to the mountains."*

The very notion of prediction seems to be unacceptable to much of scholarship.[35] Phrases such as

---

[35] Cp. Joyce Baldwin's observation that "with regard to prophecy as foretelling, the church has lost its nerve. An earthbound, rationalistic humanism has so invaded Christian thinking as to tinge with faint ridicule all claims to see in the Bible anything more than the vaguest references to future events" (*Tyndale Commentary on Daniel*, pp. 184,185). It is hard to see how there can be progress in understanding the

"morbid curiosity," using the Bible as "Old Moore's Almanac" are thrown at anyone who would be so naive as to think that Jesus could have spoken of events at least 1900 years ahead of his day. It might be conceded that He foresaw the destruction of Jersualem in A.D. 70 (although the disciples may have written the 'prophecy' after the event!), but it seems inconceivable to the commentators that Jesus could know the future beyond the first century. The whole study of prophecy has been blighted by the tendency of commentators to force biblical predictions into already fulfilled history rather than to allow that they are as yet unfulfilled.

Why should not God grant the secrets of the future to His Son, and through Him to His faithful church? It is obvious that Jesus intended his followers to gain insight into future events, since He responded directly to their question about the sign of His coming and the end of the age (Matt. 24:3). Later in the same discourse He says plainly: "Behold, I have told you in advance" (Matt. 24:25).

The reply which Jesus gave assumes that the reader will know of Daniel's forecast about the final enemy of Christianity—the Antichrist—who will set himself up as a divine authority in Jerusalem. His destruction will come at the hands of the returning Messiah. The scheme for the future described by Jesus amounts to a simple programme. There will be an 'Abomination of Desolation' (Mark's masculine participle ('standing') points to a human being, Mark 13:14), previously foreseen by Daniel (Matt. 24:15), standing in the Holy Place in Jerusalem. This is to be the cue for the Christians living in Judea to "flee

---

predictive passages of the Old Testament when commentators refuse to follow Paul's clear application of Dan. 11:36 to a future antichrist in II Thess. 2:4. Norman Porteous' commentary on *Daniel*, in the *Old Testament Library* series (p. 169), declares that "it is theologically valueless to see antichrist in Dan. 11:36." But Paul evidently did. And Jesus saw an end-of-the-age event in Dan. 11:31 (Matt. 24:15).

to the mountains," because there will follow a time of unparalleled suffering, described by Jesus as "great tribulation" (Matt. 24:21). Jesus gives specific details and warnings in connection with the flight of the Church to avoid the terrible time of distress caused by the appearance of "the Abomination of Desolation."

Immediately after this time of extreme trouble (Matt. 24:29), cosmic disturbances will occur in the sky and then the Messiah will appear in the clouds and gather His chosen people into the Kingdom of God (vv. 30, 31). As Luke puts it, "When you see [the cataclysmic events leading to the Second Coming], recognize that the Kingdom of God is near" (Luke 21:31). This critically important text supplies us with one of numerous proofs of the arrival of the Kingdom of God as an event *following* the future coming of Jesus. It should be obvious that Jesus was not talking about events in A.D. 70, immediately after which no Second Coming occurred!

The prophetic discourse of Jesus is, as He says, built on revelations granted in the sixth century B.C. to Daniel. When all the data is assembled, together with the much neglected parallel material from Isaiah, it forms a unified whole and gives a coherent picture of the future in the Middle East just prior to the Second Coming. The same subject is taken up by Paul in II Thessalonians 2, where he reinforces, against the menace of contradictory schemes designed to confuse the Church, the sequence of events given by Jesus. Paul foresees a defection from God—an apostasy—leading to the arrival and reign of the Antichrist, which is followed by the appearance of Christ in glory to destroy the final enemy, gather the faithful and establish the Kingdom (See II Thess. 2:1-12).

The material preserved for us in Jesus' Olivet discourse is all part and parcel of His messianic outlook. It cannot be divorced from the rest of His teaching without severe distortion of His (Christian) Jewish belief which has its roots in the Old Testament. This includes understanding Daniel as the medium of divine revelation concerning the future just preceding the Second Coming. [36] The book of Daniel is largely a description of the final Antichrist, of whom Antiochus Epiphanes in the second century B.C. was merely a shadow. Jesus evidently believed, as His followers also must, that the Old Testament 'antichrist,' Antiochus, provided the 'typical' groundwork for the even more sinister figure who will one day menace the saints and pose as a messianic pretender. Like Jesus, Paul took all this with the utmost seriousness and spoke of it constantly to the churches (II Thess. 2:5, "Don't you remember that while I was still with you I used to tell you these things?").

Paul saw in the Antichrist, the Man of Sin, a ghastly caricature and parody of the returning Messiah Himself. In the Apostle's view the only insurance against being duped by the fake Messiah is to be thoroughly grounded in the Truth of the divine revelation in Jesus and the scriptures (II Thess. 2:7-10). The Apostle goes so far as to say that the Antichrist will himself have a spectacular arrival, a 'parousia' (II Thess. 2:9); such will be the subtlety of Satan's efforts to deceive. In some dazzling way this pseudo-Second Coming will ape the glorious revelation of the Messiah Himself. It will be a case of opposition by imitation, leading to tragedy for those not able to discern the true from the false (II Thess. 2:10-12).

All this is basic to the New Testament outlook on the future, but it has been quite unreasonably discarded by the churches in their general neglect of New Testament Messianism. The recovery of the essential Christian teaching about the future, found throughout the New Testament, would do much to rekindle interest in biblical Christianity.

---

[36] The importance of understanding the message of the book of Daniel as a basis for understanding the teaching of Jesus can hardly be exaggerated. "Daniel among all the books of the Old Testament is...of the highest significance for the New Testament as a whole..." (H. C. Kee, *The Community of the New Age*, p. 45).

It is no exaggeration to say that the subject of Antichrist is of the utmost importance to Jesus, Paul and John, who with Luke are the principle witnesses to the apostolic faith. As we have seen, Jesus referred His disciples to the predictions of Daniel who, in chapters 7, 8, 9, 11, 12, foresaw the rise and reign of an awful tyrant, an arch-persecutor of the faithful whose dreadful career would dominate a period of seven years (the final 'heptad' of Gabriel's revelation of the seventy 'heptads' - Dan. 9:24-27), just preceding the arrival of Jesus in glory. That Jesus understood this final seven-year period to be future is shown by His placing Daniel's 'Abomination,' who is active during the seven years (Dan. 9:26, 27), in the future *immediately* before the Second Coming (Matt. 24:15, 29, 30).

The information to which Jesus refers us is found in Daniel 8:13, 9:26, 27, 11:31, 12:11 and the surrounding contexts. In these verses an abominable figure, who carries on a war of devastation and interferes with a restored temple economy, comes to his end in a 'flood' (Dan. 9:26, 11:45) or cataclysm precipitated by the arrival of Jesus "in flaming fire dealing out retribution to those who do not know God and do not obey the Gospel" (II Thess. 1:7). The event corresponds to Paul's description of the Antichrist's doom in II Thess. 2:8. From the moment the abominable tyrant is established in the holy place, there will elapse a period of about 3½ years (Dan. 12:7, 11), the second half of the final heptad of years announced by Gabriel in Dan. 9:26, 27. The book of Revelation associates the same 3½-year period with the eschatological reign of "the Beast" (Rev. 13:5).

An examination of the relevant passages in Daniel to which we are directed by Jesus in Matt. 24:15 shows that a "despicable person" (Dan. 11:21ff) will arise in the Middle East, in the area of Syria or Iraq (described as an Assyrian in Isa. 11:4, cp. II Thess. 2:8), ingratiate himself with Israel, but later turn upon them and the Christians making a final effort to establish himself in power in Jerusalem. Jesus refers quite specifically to this sequence of events, which will *immediately precede* His return (Matt. 24:29), and in Daniel's account *immediately precede* the resurrection of the faithful dead (Dan. 12:1-2). The material given us by Daniel therefore corresponds with Jesus' own development of it. Both He and Daniel describe a period of unprecedented tribulation (Dan. 12:1, Matt. 24:21) immediately prior to the end of the age. The end is marked (as everywhere else in Scripture) by the resurrection of the dead (Dan. 12:2) and by the return of Jesus (Matt. 24:29, 31). The scheme revealed by Jesus harmonizes with the clear statement of Paul about the moment when the faithful dead will be "made alive," implying, of course, that they are dead until that future moment (I Cor. 15:22). This simple plan for resurrecting the dead at the future coming of Jesus cannot be harmonized with traditional views of the dead being *already* alive with Him in heaven.

In the book of Revelation, the prophecies of Daniel and Jesus are further developed. The critical final 3½–year period of Antichrist's reign, based on Daniel 9:26, 27, 7:25, 12:7, 11 is again seen by Jesus as future (Rev. 13:5) and it comes to an end when, with the Messiah's arrival, "the kingdoms of the world have become the Kingdom of our Lord and of His Messiah, and He will reign for ever and ever" (Rev. 11:15). There then follows the long anticipated reign of Messiah and His saints, who "come to life and reign as kings with the Messiah" (Rev. 20:4).

The methods by which commentators have attempted to do away with this future Messianic Kingdom are among the most devastating in the whole history of mishandling the words of Scripture. The resurrection of previously beheaded saints to reign with Jesus (Rev. 20:4) can, of course, refer only to a real resurrection from the dead. It certainly cannot be a description of Christian conversion now! Yet this has been the traditional view since Augustine, and it is a witness to the whole antimessianic tendency of traditional Christianity.

The "first resurrection" (Rev. 20:5), describing the blessedness of those who come to life in order to be "priests of God and the Messiah and reign with Him for a thousand years" (Rev. 20:6), follows the Second Coming seen by John in Revelation 19:11-21. The order of events is just what we would expect from the sequence given by Paul in I Cor. 15:22, 23. After being made alive by resurrection, the faithful embark on their reign with the Messiah, exactly as Jesus had promised in the texts we have already discussed (Matt. 19:18, Luke 22:28-30, Rev. 2:26, 3:21, 5:10).

A careful collation of the extensive material provided by the prophecies of Daniel, Isaiah, Paul and Jesus Himself in the Gospel and Revelation provides us with a rather detailed picture of events in the region of Israel leading to the return of the Messiah. A much neglected feature of Paul's account of the Antichrist in II Thess. 2 is his quotation from Isaiah 11:4. The reference there is to an end-time Assyrian, further described in Isaiah 30:27-32:4 in a messianic setting, "whom the Lord Jesus will slay with the breath of his mouth and bring to an end by the appearance of his coming" (II Thess. 2:8). As is well known, the ruler of Assyria is to be found in the territory formerly held by the Assyrian and Babylonian empires, now by Iraq. It is from that quarter that scripture seems to expect the Antichrist to arise; and it is most likely that the whole of Daniel 11, from v. 5 onwards, is a prediction of events yet future to our time. As history they are sometimes both sketchy and erratic and, despite some parallels, do not correspond exactly with the succession of Syrian kings who lived in the fourth to the second century B.C. The narrative from Dan. 11:5 through to Dan. 12:3 reads as a connected whole, much of which corresponds to nothing in history, while the remainder has been only imperfectly fulfilled. The great revelation granted to Daniel in chapters 10-12 to show him "what will happen to your people at the end of the days, [i.e., the days just preceding the Messianic Kingdom] for the vision pertains to the days yet future" should be treasured by all those who take seriously Jesus' admonition to read and understand the book of Daniel. (See Dan. 10:14 and Jesus' instructions in Matt. 24:15.)

The prophecy is clearly granted to the church as a comfort in the difficult last days before Messiah's return. Jesus' reference to the Abomination of Desolation in Dan. 9:27, 11:31, 12:11 directs our attention to the whole context in which these verses are found. This is exactly the New Testament method.

> "When the N.T. quotes a brief O.T. passage, it often applies implicitly to the entire context of the quotation" (*Expositor's Bible Commentary on Matthew*, D. A. Carson, p. 205).

'Scholarship' has been unwilling to follow Jesus or Paul closely when it comes to their preoccupation with the (to them) distant future preceding the Second Coming. However, there is no logical reason to treat any less seriously the forecast of future events given by Jesus in Matthew 24 than one would, for example, the sermon on the mount. 'Theology' seems to have done its best to divorce Jesus from what is viewed as the 'unsuitable' teaching contained in the Olivet discourse. The New Testament, however, presents the Son of God as no less authoritative in His prediction of the future than in his radical ethical demands. All is a reflection of the Messiah's messianic outlook and belief. Every bit of the New Testament data is required in order to give us a rounded picture of the Jesus of history and faith.

Churches, therefore, cannot claim to represent the mind of Jesus unless they convey to their members and the world the sum of all that Jesus taught.[37]   It

---

[37]   James Barr observes that "traditional orthodoxy is a monumental example of the 'picking and choosing' that it deprecates in others. Actually 'liberal' theology in its emphasis on (say) the Kingdom of God was following the canonical

is clear that traditional Christians have simply
neglected or suppressed major parts of this teaching.[38]
In their selective treatment of the records, churches
appear to endorse only what tradition will permit.
Much of the rest of what Jesus taught has been
pushed aside as 'Jewish' or 'unspiritual.' There is a
persistent anti-Semitic streak in traditional theology.
It is Jesus *Christ's* (and therefore by definition
Christian) Messianism which has suffered so disastrously
from uncomprehending Gentile commentary.

---

proportions of the Gospels much more faithfully" (*Holy Scripture, Canon Authority Criticism*, p. 40). Unfortunately the
'liberals' understood the Kingdom of God quite differently from
Jesus. Bultmann dismissed the entire New Testament hope for the
future, cancelling the future Kingdom of God with a single
stroke: "We can no longer look for the return of the Son of Man
on the clouds of Heaven, or hope that the faithful will meet him
in the air" (*Kerygma and Myth*, p. 4).

38   In 1926, William Temple, Archbishop of Canterbury, noted
that "the great discovery of the age in which we live is the
immense prominence given in the Gospel to the Kingdom of God.
To us it is quite extraordinary that it figures so little in the
theology and religious writings of almost the entire period of
Christian history. Certainly in the synoptic Gospels it has a
prominence that could hardly be increased" (*Personal Religion
and the Life of Fellowship*, p. 69). Since the Gospel is the
Gospel *of the Kingdom,* its absence from theology means the loss
of the Gospel.

Conclusion

B. F. Westcott was undoubtedly right:

"It is not enough to recognize that the Old Testament contains prophecies; the Old Testament is one vast prophecy."

A large part of that prophecy deals with the Messianic Kingdom in its final manifestation as a worldwide government under the supervision of Jesus and the faithful Christians. It is that Kingdom, we believe, which forms the heart of the Christian Gospel and it is that Kingdom which is largely absent from received systems of what we know as Christian theology.

Surely Rodolf Otto's analysis is correct:

"The Kingdom of God is and remains for Christ the future Kingdom of the final age, thought of in strictly eschatological terms, following on the 'messianic woes' following on the Divine Judgement" (*The Kingdom of God and the Son of Man*, p. 10).

We know that the 'messianic woes' remained future in Jesus' thinking (Matt. 24:8—"These are the beginning of birth pangs"). They were to be the prelude to the arrival of the Kingdom, whose preparation in the present age is the subject of the parables. The Word of the Kingdom is sown in the heart now (Matt. 13:19). The Christian is to become "a disciple of the Kingdom" (Matt. 13:52). The harvest born by the Message is reaped at the end of the age, when the genuine sons of the Kingdom will shine forth in the Kingdom of their Father (Matt. 13:43). It is true that the faithful can experience something of the miracle of the Kingdom now, in advance of the coming of the Kingdom. They are an advance guard, heralding the Good News of a better world to come— but one which is a real human society, renewed and reeducated, and in the hands of immortalized adminis- trators. "How shall we escape if we neglect so great a salvation...for He has not subjected to angels the inhabited world to come of which we speak" (Heb. 2:5). Would that contemporary church-goers could speak that kind of language and know what they were saying—for He *has* placed that future world in the hands of Jesus and the faithful Church. The world is "not yet" under Jesus' control but it is destined to come under His jurisdiction when He returns (Heb. 2:5, 8).

It is a bizarre system of exposition which can accuse the Apostles of blindness for their Jewish- Christian Messianism when, in Acts 1:6, they enquired about the restoration of the Kingdom to Israel. The question was put by the Apostles on the eve of Pente- cost after they had been fully informed by Jesus who "explained everything privately to His disciples" (Mark 4:34). Jesus had earlier assured Himself that they had fully understood the Kingdom (Matt. 13:51). At the Last Supper He formally covenanted with them to grant them positions of royalty in the coming divine rule (Luke 22:28-30). For six weeks after His resurrection they were again instructed in "the things concerning the Kingdom of God" (Acts 1:3). On the basis of all they had heard and understood, they asked whether the time had now come for the restoration of the Kingdom to Israel. It is the right question, not, as so many commentators try to persuade us, a horrible mistake!

"The form of the question itself reflects the common Jewish idea of the Messiah's kingdom, and shows how far the apostles still were from real insight into the nature of their

Master's mission. How incredible it is that these men should have been instructed during 40 days and had not even ceased to expect...an earthly Jewish empire in which they themselves should hold high places around the Messiah's person.... It is a mark of the author's candour that he records such a mistaken idea of the apostles in their earlier days" (*The Century Bible*, Acts, p. 126).

It is indeed incredible and impossible that the Apostles should have been mistaken about the nature of the Kingdom which had been the heart of all that Jesus had taught them! Nothing, here or elsewhere, suggests that Jesus disapproved of their hope for a 'concrete' Kingdom of God on earth. The *time* for the restoration was not known, and the path to greatness in the Kingdom was through humility, sacrifice and service, *but the reality of the future Kingdom was never in question*. Indeed, only a few days later, we find the Apostles proclaiming the Gospel to the Jewish people under the influence of the spirit of God. They still believed in the great restoration which was the burden of all that the prophets had seen:

> "*Heaven must receive Jesus until the times of the restoration of all things, of which times all the prophets have spoken*" *(Acts 3:21).*

There is no dramatic new understanding of the Kingdom. The Kingdom remains the Kingdom of Hebrew prophecy which, but for nearly 1800 years of anti-messianic commentary, would have been clearly understood by ordinary readers of the Bible.[39]   It is

---

[39] The reality of the future Messianic Kingdom was removed from theology largely by Augustine who "pushed it completely into the background and replaced it by another scheme of eschatology, which since the fifth century, has been regarded more or less as the orthodox teaching" (P. Toon, "Introduction", *Puritan Eschatology*, p. 13).

high time for scholars and preachers to abandon their unwarranted opposition to Jesus, the Messiah of Israel, and to join Him in announcing the Good News about the Kingdom. Critics must also come to see that their scepticism is an attack on the core of the Christian Gospel:

> "The coming of the transcendental Son of Man to achieve the catastrophic transformation of the present aeon, or order...has proved to be one of the beliefs about man and the world and their history which Jesus shared with His contemporaries and which time and the advance of knowledge have left behind as the relics of a bygone mentality" (James McKinnon, *The Historic Jesus*, p. 207).

If that really is the case, Jesus was sadly mistaken and can be safely dismissed as a false prophet. But the fault lies with the unbelieving commentators, whose aversion to the Messianism of the New Testament has resulted in their rejection of the whole promise of the Kingdom:

> "The Messiah, whose birth the angel proclaimed, is depicted in the form of a king who shall occupy and hold for ever the throne of His father (ancestor) David. A restored Jewish kingdom is predicted, and this prediction ultimately proved not only an illusion, but incompatible with the spiritual kingdom which Jesus proclaimed and sought to establish.... The angelic communication, under the influence of current belief, is based on a misconception of historic reality. It is, to say the least, rather disconcerting to find what purports to be a revelation from a heavenly source misinterpreting a prophecy and also predicting a restored Davidic kingdom which failed to materialize" (ibid., pp. 5, 6).

In other words, "Poor old Gabriel! He got it all

wrong." And so, adds the chorus of commentators, did the disciples when they still expected that 'Jewish' Kingdom in Acts 1:6. But then Jesus Himself, it would seem, was also in the dark about the Kingdom when He promised His followers positions of authority over Israel (Luke 22:28-30) and urged them to strive for rulership with Him in the coming new era (Rev. 2:26, 3:21).

Expositors of the Bible, and indeed the entire traditional Christian system, urgently need a new orientation. We must cease mounting our own tradition against the word of God,[40] and return to the messianic Good News of the Kingdom and to belief in Jesus, the Jewish Christ, Saviour of the world, now exalted to the right hand of His Father and destined to return and rule as Messiah and King. "Even so, Lord Jesus, come!"

---

[40] Is Jesus' criticism of traditions which nullify the divine Word any less relevant today? (Matt. 15:8, 9.)